THIS BOOK
BELONGS TO

_____

A
LITTLE
GOD
TIME

FOR
Mothers

365 DAILY DEVOTIONS

BroadStreet
PUBLISHING

BroadStreet Publishing Group LLC
Savage, Minnesota, USA
Broadstreetpublishing.com

A Little God Time for Mothers

© 2021 by BroadStreet Publishing®

978-1-4245-6222-0 (faux)

Devotional entries composed by Cari Dugan, Laura Krause, Stephanie Sample, Jacquelyn Senske, and Michelle Winger.

All rights reserved. No part of this publication may be reproduced, distributed, or transmitted in any form or by any means, including photocopying, recording, or other electronic or mechanical methods, without the prior written permission of the publisher, except in the case of brief quotations embodied in critical reviews and certain other noncommercial uses permitted by copyright law.

Scripture quotations marked (NLT) are taken from the Holy Bible, New Living Translation, copyright © 1996, 2004, 2007. Used by permission of Tyndale House Publishers, Inc., Carol Stream, Illinois 60188. All rights reserved. Scripture quotations marked (NIV) are taken from the Holy Bible, New International Version®, niv®. Copyright © 1973, 1978, 1984, 2011 by Biblica, Inc.™ Used by permission of Zondervan. All rights reserved worldwide. www.zondervan.com. The "niv" and "New International Version" are trademarks registered in the United States Patent and Trademark Office by Biblica, Inc.™ Scripture quotations marked (NCV) are taken from the New Century Version®. Copyright © 2005 by Thomas Nelson. Used by permission. All rights reserved. Scripture quotations marked (NASB) are taken from the New American Standard Bible®, Copyright © 1960, 1962, 1963, 1968, 1971, 1972, 1973, 1975, 1977, 1995 by The Lockman Foundation. Used by permission. www.Lockman.org. Scripture quotations marked (NRSV) are taken from the New Revised Standard Version Bible, copyright 1989, Division of Christian Education of the National Council of the Churches of Christ in the United States of America. Used by permission. All rights reserved. Scripture quotations marked (ESV) are from the esv® Bible (The Holy Bible, English Standard Version®), copyright © 2001 by Crossway, a publishing ministry of Good News Publishers. Used by permission. All rights reserved. Scripture quotations marked (NKJV) are taken from the New King James Version®. Copyright © 1982 by Thomas Nelson. Used by permission. All rights reserved. Scripture quotations marked (TPT) are taken from The Passion Translation® of the Holy Bible. Copyright © 2017, 2018 by Passion & Fire Ministries Inc. Used by permission of BroadStreet Publishing. All rights reserved.

Design by Chris Garborg | garborgdesign.com
Edited and compiled by Michelle Winger | literallyprecise.com

Printed in China.

21 22 23 24 25 7 6 5 4 3 2 1

She speaks with wisdom,

and faithful instruction is on her tongue.

She watches over the affairs of her household

and does not eat the bread of idleness.

Her children arise and call her blessed.

PROVERBS 31:26-28 NIV

Introduction

When life demands your attention, carve out a little God time and find a few moments of peace. A little quiet time is what all mothers need but can rarely find in the craziness of everyday life.

Be encouraged as you reflect on these devotions, Scriptures, and prayers each day. As you spend some time with God, you will find the grace and strength needed to get through all your day holds. The blessing of motherhood is found in the middle of the hard work.

Allow joy and peace to flood your heart as you rest in God and endeavor to love your children the way he loves you. You can be confident that every act of service and sacrifice will be rewarded one day.

January

"So do not fear, for I am with you;

do not be dismayed, for I am your God.

I will strengthen you and help you;

I will uphold you with my righteous right hand."

ISAIAH 41:10 NIV

Break Every Chain

He has done this so that every person would long for God,
feel their way to him,[a] and find him—
for he is the God who is easy to discover!
ACTS 17:27 TPT

There is a chance to start over every day if we need to. From the inside out, we can be transformed and our hearts renewed. We can essentially remake ourselves with the help, healing, and transformative nature of Christ! Jesus died on the cross to promise us a life free from the bondage of sin, free from hopelessness, free from any chains that try to trap us. In Christ, we are set free.

We need to hear the truth of Christ's promise for us and stop the cycle of hopelessness, defeat, and bondage to sin. All we need to do is get on our knees and pray.

Is there an area of your life that you need to repent of and receive freedom from? Wait for God's voice to permeate the deepest, saddest parts of you. He wants you to live a life where he takes care of you. He desires a relationship with you. He is pursuing your heart. He is pursuing all of you.

Letting Go

"I tell you, do not worry about your life, what you will eat or drink; or about your body, what you will wear. Is not life more than food, and the body more than clothes? Look at the birds of the air; they do not sow or reap or store away in barns, and yet your heavenly Father feeds them. Are you not much more valuable than they? Can any one of you by worrying add a single hour to your life?"

MATTHEW 6:25-27 NIV

Of all the things God asks us to let go of, for a mother, worry just might be the most difficult. From little things like running out of milk or forgetting to do that load of laundry, to genuine concerns such as the first time our kids go away for a weekend, put on a football helmet, or get behind the wheel, we are tempted to give in to worry.

God desires our trust! He wants us to surrender—ourselves and our precious children—to him and his perfect plan. He wants us to rest in his love, and he promises to care for us.

What worry or fear are you holding on to?
What would it take for you to open your hand and give it over to God?

Misplaced Security

"Don't let your hearts be troubled.
Trust in God, and trust also in me."
JOHN 14:1 NLT

It is normal for moms to manage a million things all at the same time. A part of us likes to have control because it gives us a sense of security. But is that security false? What happens when circumstances are out of our control? When relationships are broken, our children are sick, or there just isn't enough money in the bank to cover mounting bills? We allow worry to seep into our hearts. We become anxious and insecure. More often than not, we allow our concerns to debilitate us—to rob us from our sleep and kill our joy.

We don't have to become weary if we remember that we serve a God who loves us so much that he wants us to shrug off the burdens that make us ache and trust him instead. Regardless of the situation and circumstance, God is in control. Our security rests in him and not in our own abilities. The next time life sends you a curve ball, instead of succumbing to fear and scrambling to maintain control, bring your concerns to the one who listens and cares deeply.

What are you worried about today?
Talk to God and leave it all in his hands.

Forgiveness Circle

"If you forgive those who sin against you,
your heavenly Father will forgive you.
But if you refuse to forgive others,
your Father will not forgive your sins."

MATTHEW 6:14-15 NLT

Many of us long-ago memorized a version of the prayer Jesus gave us in Matthew 6 and have repeated it hundreds or thousands of times. Many have taught it to their children as well. We ask for God to be glorified, for just enough food for today, to be forgiven the way we forgive, and to be protected from temptation. "That's all you need to say," Jesus tells us.

Wait. Back up. To be forgiven how? Since we are all sinners, God's grace is what we count on. Our lives depend on his forgiveness. Just to make sure we got the point, after sharing the prayer in verses 9-13, he follows up with the Scripture above.

How are you teaching your children the importance of forgiveness? According to Jesus, there's only one way to get it, and that is to give it. How is this principle working in your own life?

Summer and Winter

The day is yours, and yours also the night;
you established the sun and moon.
It was you who set all the boundaries of the earth;
you made both summer and winter.
PSALM 74:16-17 NIV

Those who live in a cold climate understand that winters can get long. As the amount of daylight decreases, it's easy to find discouragement or depression creeping in. Sometimes this is a direct result of just needing more vitamin D to compensate for the lack of sunlight. But sometimes the Lord allows this to drive you to a place of finding a deeper degree of contentment in him.

God created the seasons. They are his making. Winter treasures are like manna; the same manna would be rotten in the summer. Manna that is provided on a daily basis refreshes us and provides the kind of nourishment we need.

Are you making the most out of this season or living in complaint? Don't wish away winter. There are treasures there for the taking. If you seek them, they will be found.

Working Hard

Whatever you do, do your work heartily,
as for the Lord rather than for men.
COLOSSIANS 3:23 NASB

What is at the core of our motivations? We all have things that motivate us and reasons why we work hard. We are easily motivated by money, affirmation, and admiration. We might want prestigious titles or big promotions.

As mothers, why do we put our hearts and souls into our families? There is no financial gain, and rarely do we receive affirmation or thanks. Do we do our best so that the world thinks we are good mothers? So that our children like and appreciate us? So that the world will admire our efforts?

What motivates you? Do you work hard because that is what is expected of you, or do you work hard to serve and please God? Whatever you do, do it happily in worship to the Lord. He is the giver of your talents and abilities. He is the strength for your work and the center of your creative inspiration.

Short Years

May the Lord lead your hearts into a full understanding and expression of the love of God and the patient endurance that comes from Christ.
2 THESSALONIANS 3:5 NLT

Motherhood is such a gift. It requires selflessness. It requires work. It tests your patience. And sometimes, the days feel really long. But the days that you are knee-deep in diapers and up at all hours of the night go quickly. Soon you will be entrusting others to care for your children, and eventually asking your children to take care of themselves. So, hard-working mothers, embrace all that motherhood brings: the beautiful and the hard, the days of laughter and the days of sickness, the days of play and the days of work, the moments of joy and the moments of frustration.

Through all of the years, we know that Jesus is walking alongside us. In every moment, no matter the circumstance, he is there; laughing along with us and wiping away our tears. Motherhood is a gift—a privilege. It is honoring and life-giving.

Do you frequently experience the ups and downs of motherhood? Remember in the moments of weakness and moments of joy, that motherhood truly is a gift. And remember who is right beside through it all.

Distracted Parenting

The Spirit of the LORD will rest on him—
the Spirit of wisdom and understanding.
ISAIAH 11:2 NLT

God isn't asking you to be a perfect mom. He is the only perfect parent. He isn't alarmed by your inadequacies. He knew you would sin, which is why he provided his son as a sacrifice for you to be restored to him when you confess. But there are simple steps you can take to become a better parent.

Have we allowed distractions into our world that are hindering our ability to parent? Some of these distractions could have begun with a well-meaning heart. Perhaps we had questions on how to parent. Now we have found that we are up to our eyeballs in mommy blogs with no answers and more questions. Many times these helpful tools hinder us from going to the one who has every answer we ever could need. He knows our children better than we do; therefore, he knows the way to parent them. We only have to ask.

Have you become a victim of distracted parenting? Have you sought the Father for wisdom in parenting before asking the world? He is more than willing to share his heart with you.

Fearing God

In the fear of the LORD there is strong confidence,
And his children will have refuge.
PROVERBS 14:26 NASB

A child is blessed to have a mother who habitually goes to the feet of God in petition for wisdom. There is security in having a mother who seeks knowledge in parenting God's way and not in the world's way. Mothers who pray for their children and continually put their trust in the Lord create a wonderful atmosphere and safe home for children to grow up in.

Children who grow up seeing their mother trusting in Jesus and seeking him to direct their paths eventually learn to have confidence in God's leading. A mother's example to love and obey God is a wonderful gift to her children.

Do you have the fear of God in your home? Do you ask for his wisdom and trust that he will lead you? Take heart, Mom! By entrusting your life to God, you are entrusting your child to his faithful hands as well.

No Guidebook

Oh, the depth of the riches both of the wisdom and knowledge of God!
How unsearchable are His judgments and unfathomable His ways!
ROMANS 11:33 NASB

Do you remember those early days as a new mom? However God blessed you with a child, there were likely a couple of terrifying first few moments. One minute it is just you, and the next, there's this tiny being you're suddenly responsible for. Your heart is flooded with love, but your hands have no idea what to do. A guidebook would have been nice.

There are a million parenting books available, blogs to read, and advice to collect from family and friends who have gone before us on this parenting journey, but we still have to figure it out for ourselves. Before we know it, we do. We don't perfect it, but we're parents. We're certifiable women responsible for another little person, and he or she is surviving just fine. Because really, our guidebook for parenting is love. No matter how often our babies are eating, or how many hours they are sleeping at night, our little ones are loved. That is not only surviving, that is thriving.

Can you see how far you've come in loving your children?

Don't Be Anxious

Give your burdens to the LORD,
and he will take care of you.
PSALM 55:22 NLT

God is serious when he tells us not to be anxious. He isn't just giving us a suggestion. He is telling us of one of the many privileges we have as his daughters: the gift of never having to worry. Unfortunately, many of us still think we are accomplishing something by worrying; therefore, we continue it.

God alone knows what tomorrow holds, and he knows that we can't alter anything by worrying about it. Furthermore, we weren't made to sustain anxiety. Our bodies weren't built to endure it. This is why worry and anxiety can make us physically sick. Nothing delights God more than a child that demonstrates their trust in his goodness and provision by choosing not to worry about tomorrow.

Did you know that it is an action of great faith and trust not to worry? Trust isn't for the faint of heart. It is an act of maturity. It is a pure, childlike action that takes courage. But know that it is what God intends for you. Ask the Father to help you find the childlike place of trust in him.

Presence and Protection

God is in the midst of her;
she shall not be moved;
God will help her when morning dawns.
PSALM 46:5 ESV

Often our culture threatens to destroy the sanctity of family and home. A home that centers around Christ is not easily shaken, nor can it be destroyed. We have nothing to fear because what is God's cannot be destroyed. He reigns and triumphs over anything that tries to take you down.

We can invite God into our homes. Make him Lord over our families. Trust him because he holds us. Our families are untouchable with God's protection. In all times of trouble, God will be there.

God dwells in the city that cannot be destroyed. Does he dwell in your home? There is safety in trusting him with your life and home. Giving him presence in your family and house invites his protection as well.

Childlike Faith

"I thank you, Father, Lord of heaven and earth,
that you have hidden these things from the wise and understanding
and revealed them to little children."

MATTHEW 11:25 ESV

There are many things we can learn from our children. Jesus taught this when the disciples were asking him who would be the greatest in the kingdom of heaven. We don't know definitively why they were asking, but we can make the assumption that they weren't at all expecting the answer Jesus gave. He brought a child into their midst and said that unless they became like a child, they would never enter the kingdom of heaven.

A child's faith in God knows no doubt. They believe—quite simply—that he is who he says he is and he will do what he says he will do. They aren't discouraged, and they have no reason to doubt his faithfulness. God challenges us to have that kind of faith: sincere and pure.

Can you ask God for faith that doesn't give up?
In spite of discouragement, you can trust him like a child would.
Contend for that kind of faith in your heart.

Control the Chaos

This God—his way is perfect;
the word of the LORD proves true;
he is a shield for all those who take refuge in him.

2 SAMUEL 22:31 ESV

Much of our life feels like a chaotic whirlwind that might never stop; running from activity to activity; washing, drying, and folding what feels like a hundred loads of laundry; cooking meal after meal; stopping fight after fight; cleaning room after room; the list of chaos goes on. With that chaos comes a choice: be crazy in our attitude toward everyone around us, or choose peace. There is an obvious winner.

The chaos of life is what it is. It will be there as long as we have kids, jobs, and houses to run. It can either be embraced as part of life, minimizing the control it will actually have on who we are, or we can buy into the race, giving chaos the control. Choose not to let chaos win.

What tangible things can you do to embrace the busy, chaotic times in life and remember what truly matters? Don't let chaos gain control of a life that is filled with abundant blessings from the Father who loves you and intricately created you.

Daily Compass

Guide me in your truth and teach me,
for you are God my Savior,
and my hope is in you all day long.
PSALM 25:5 NIV

Starting our day with his truth impressed on our hearts serves as a compass for our daily life. His Spirit floods ours with love, goodness, compassion, and understanding. God's whispered reminders allow us to gain perspective in our situations and help us deal with them in the most empathetic way possible.

We serve a gentle and humble Father, a Father who loves us in ways we can't even grasp. He promises communion with him whenever we need it. But this relationship goes two ways. As much as we need his Spirit to serve as our compass, he desires our attention, love, and praise right back.

Do you take dedicated time to thank God for all he is in your life? Think of a moment you shared with your children when they said something like, "I love you, Mommy; thank you for all you do." Imagine your heavenly Father and the joy it brings him when you praise him for his faithfulness.

Calm in the Storm

Soon a fierce storm came up.
High waves were breaking into the boat, and it began to fill with water.
Jesus was sleeping at the back of the boat with his head on a cushion.
The disciples woke him up, shouting, "Teacher,
don't you care that we're going to drown?"
When Jesus woke up, he rebuked the wind and said to the waves,
"Silence! Be still!" Suddenly the wind stopped,
and there was a great calm. Then he asked them,
"Why are you afraid? Do you still have no faith?"
MARK 4:37-40 NLT

Think about the scariest storm you've ever experienced. Are there days—or even weeks—when your life reminds you of that storm? Obligations pelt your skin like sleet, pressures swirl around you like the January wind, and bills come at you like a tornado.

Only angry clouds are visible everywhere we look. What about little storms: a sick kid the day of a deadline, or a forgotten carpool trip? Where do we go for peace?

Even if skies are blue in your world today, you know a storm will come eventually. Will you seek safety and comfort from the one who calmed the sea, or will you paddle furiously on your own? With a few words, Jesus quieted the storm. He ended it. Have you ever asked him to do this for you, believing he could?

Escape from Battle

No temptation has overtaken you except what is common to mankind. And God is faithful; he will not let you be tempted beyond what you can bear. But when you are tempted, he will also provide a way out so that you can endure it.

1 CORINTHIANS 10:13 NIV

Maybe you wrestle with anger or greed. Perhaps your struggle is with pride or vanity. It could be that you find it difficult to be honest or kind. Whatever your battle, you don't battle alone. We all have struggles, but God will not allow us to struggle with something too big to conquer.

We can be confident in every battle, in every struggle, and in every temptation, God will give us a way out. An escape plan is ready. When we face temptation, we can ask God for his help. He is faithful, and he will answer our cry.

What battles do you face today? Cry out to him and have faith that he will rescue you. He won't abandon you; instead, he will strengthen you.

The Labor Cycle

Never become tired of doing good.
2 Thessalonians 3:13 ncv

Often the labor of a mother is cyclical. There are many chores that need to be repeated daily. There are three meals that need to be prepared with two or three snacks in between. There are crumbs on the floor, jelly splotches on the counter, and Sippy cups that need to be washed— every day. There is laundry that literally never ends. And after the house gets put back together, the rooms get straightened, and the kids go to sleep, we end our day knowing that many of those same chores will be repeated again tomorrow. Dear mothers, it is easy to grow weary.

Weariness can seep in if we fix our eyes purely on the work set before us. The chores will be required of us tomorrow; we cannot change that. But what we can change is what our eyes are fixed upon. We can fix them on Jesus instead of our labors.

Do you feel weary when you think of all you have to do each day? When your eyes are fixed on him, praise will arise from your heart and lips. You will no longer despise your work; you will enjoy it because you are simultaneously enjoying his presence.

One Master

"No one can serve two masters.
Either you will hate the one and love the other,
or you will be devoted to the one and despise the other."
MATTHEW 6:24 NIV

We cannot serve two masters. We just can't. Our masters can look very different depending on our lives. One master is God and our relationship with him. The other? It might be our family, wealth, social status, friends, work, hobbies, or food. It's something that sits on the cusp of dominating our lives.

We can't serve both masters equally; one has to be placed second. If we spend our time and energy on serving God, if we devote ourselves to him, we will reap great eternal reward. But if we choose to serve anything other than him, if we devote ourselves to that other master—whatever it is—we will lose in the end.

What master are you serving with the way you live your life?
Choose wisely today! Choose to serve the master that matters—
the one who loves and cares about you.

The Offender's Heart

As those who have been chosen of God, holy and beloved, put on a heart of compassion, kindness, humility, gentleness and patience; bearing with one another, and forgiving each other, whoever has a complaint against anyone; just as the Lord forgave you, so also should you.
COLOSSIANS 3:12-13 NASB

When someone hurts us deeply, it isn't easy to look past the offense and look into the offender's heart. But that is exactly what God does for us, and he wants us to do the same for others. Again, and again, and again. More often than not, we will discover the offender drowning in their own sea of hurt and despair. They, too, need a great measure of love.

If we ask God to see our offenders the way he views them, we will develop a deep understanding and compassion for them. Our hurts may even pale in comparison to their pain. We see that they are lost and desire someone to help them. We give them kindness and grace, just as God gave us kindness and grace.

Are you having difficulty showing grace and compassion to someone in your life that has hurt you? Ask God to change your heart toward your offender.

Qualified for the Job

Whatever you do, work at it with all your heart, as working for the Lord, not for human masters, since you know that you will receive an inheritance from the Lord as a reward. It is the Lord Christ you are serving.
COLOSSIANS 3:23-24 NIV

Whether "Mom" is your only title or one of several, the day you became a mother you took on a full-time job with crazy hours, non-existent pay, and inconsistent benefits. Some days, it's the greatest gift in the world to love and serve our families. On others, we find ourselves wondering, Does this job get any easier? Any better?

On those days with more responsibilities than time, more grumbling than gratitude, rest in this: your employer is not that tantrum-throwing toddler or eye-rolling teenager. God chose you specifically for this family; you were the only candidate for the job, and you are perfectly qualified. You work for him, and he will give you all the support, recognition, and joy you need.

What part of your work as a mother is the most difficult for you? Share your struggles with God. Does it help you to remember you are working for him at a job he chose just for you?

Unforgotten Benefits

Bless the LORD, O my soul,
and all that is within me,
bless his holy name!
Bless the LORD, O my soul,
and forget not all his benefits.
PSALM 103:1-2 ESV

Have you ever noticed the raw humanity of David in the psalms? David is known for the many exploits that he performed courageously. He killed a lion, a bear, and a giant! But the psalms offer us a glimpse into David's heart between his valiant battles. He continually wrestled with his own heart and sin. He wrote of the attributes he knew to be true of God only to follow it up with phrases asking how long the Lord would forget him.

We should not berate ourselves for faith that one day makes us feel like we could slay a giant and the next day we wonder if God even hears our prayers. We are human. What we can do, on those rough days, is take time to remember who he says he is.

Do you feel like you are prone to forget the benefits of God even if you seemed to know them an hour ago? Take time to ponder the attributes of God. In doing so, he will lift your head.

A Pillar

*The L*ORD *is my rock and my fortress and my deliverer,*
My God, my rock, in whom I take refuge;
My shield and the horn of my salvation, my stronghold.
PSALM 18:2 NASB

We never know how we will react when tragedy strikes, when we are beyond our understanding, or when we are faced with an unshakeable circumstance. What can we do to prepare ourselves? Not much in the physical world. But we can prune our hearts. We can ask for total dependence on our Father. We can more fully understand how deep and wide and long his love is for us, so that when we are faced with uncertainty, we cling to what we know is certain—Jesus.

Jesus is our ultimate support. He is our rock. He is our pillar of strength when we feel unsteady and uncertain. When we question, he is our answer. When we cry out for help, he is our comfort. When we ask why, he whispers his truth of a plan for our lives.

What do you think you would cling to in a circumstance that's beyond your understanding? Allow yourself to fall so deeply in love with Jesus that you know nothing else except how to live a life for him.

Comparisons

A peaceful heart leads to a healthy body;
jealousy is like cancer in the bones.
PROVERBS 14:30 NLT

Comparing your life to your friend's life is dangerous. Even the best of us get caught doing it if we aren't careful to guard our hearts. "She has a better job, a bigger house, and a luxurious family vacation every year. My house is tiny, my job is horrid, and we never get to go on vacation!" Sound familiar?

Jealousy can eat us up inside, leaving us bitter, hardhearted, and cold. Greed and envy can ruin a beautiful friendship. There will always be someone else that has more than we do. Choosing to be content with where we are in life will bring us peace. It will also allow us to genuinely celebrate the fortunes and blessings of others, partaking in their joy. This is a wonderful thing.

Are you envious of a friend or neighbor?
How can you choose to be content with what you have?

Light to the Eyes

How long must I wrestle with my thoughts
and day after day have sorrow in my heart?
How long will my enemy triumph over me?
Look on me and answer, LORD my God.
Give light to my eyes, or I will sleep in death,
and my enemy will say, "I have overcome him,"
and my foes will rejoice when I fall.
But I trust in your unfailing love;
my heart rejoices in your salvation.
I will sing the LORD's praise,
for he has been good to me.
PSALM 13:2-6 NIV

God can help us see life through his eyes. He can bring us beyond our feelings to see the truth about the situation we are facing. We serve a loving Father who longs to see us rejoicing and recognizing the faithfulness of his love for us.

There is no situation too difficult for him, no trial he can't overcome, no amount of unloving action on our part that can ever sway him from desiring a relationship with us.

What situation do you need discernment about today?
Ask God to give light to your eyes. If nothing else today, let him impress upon your heart a measure of his unfailing love for you.

Volume Down

Don't use foul or abusive language.
Let everything you say be good and helpful,
so that your words will be an encouragement to those who hear them.
EPHESIANS 4:29 NLT

Without a doubt, one of the toughest tasks of motherhood is keeping our cool when our children are out of line. How do we model patience and lovingkindness when they are pushing our buttons—hard?

For being such adorable creatures, kids sure can inspire a surprising amount of anger in us, can't they? And that anger can occasionally (or maybe even often) be accompanied by yelling and saying things we wish we hadn't said. It never really helps the situation, does it? When we lose it, we lose sight of our intention to build our children up. We add pain and distance to an already difficult situation.

How do you feel after you yell at your kids? How do they feel? The next time you feel that loud, angry voice bubbling up inside you, remember Ephesians 4:29. Ask the Holy Spirit to give you words of encouragement or the strength to walk away until you feel more in control. And when the inevitable happens and you lose it anyway, forgive yourself. Remember, his mercies are new every morning.

Fasting

"He must increase,
but I must decrease."
JOHN 3:30 ESV

There are plenty of things that God alone does in our lives. There are things that only he is able to heal and deliver us from. However, there are also areas in our lives that the Lord would love to move in, but he wants us to partner with him to do so. One of the ways he does this is by inviting us to fast.

Fasting is intentionally not eating food for a period of time whether it is for a meal, a day, or a week. God uses fasting to strengthen us spiritually. When we take time to intentionally not "feed" a primal need so that we might lean into him and get strength from him, we will find our internal strength increases. If we can regularly practice not eating food when we are hungry, we find that our strength and ability to say no to a particular sin also increases.

Do you know that fasting is a tangible way to embrace weakness so that God might increase in you? Even if your effort is feeble, rest assured God will honor you for it.

Fighter Mom

We will not hide these truths from our children;
we will tell the next generation
about the glorious deeds of the LORD,
about his power and his mighty wonders.
PSALM 78:4 NLT

Your kids will undoubtedly encounter trials in life. It could be peer pressure at school, strife with friendships, or just figuring out how to set a Godly example in a secular world. While they are growing in maturity of their faith, this is a reminder to fight for your kids, not against them. Fight for them like God fights for you every day.

Whether we can grasp it or not, we were specifically chosen to be the mother of the kids we have. They are God's precious ones entrusted to our care. We have to stand firm in the truth and lay aside our personal opinions. Our kids need someone to fight for them and God has called us to be the fighters.

Have you fought for your kids lately, or are you always fighting against them? Make it a point to contend for them. After all, you're their mom. It always helps to have your mom on your side.

Gift of Perspective

To everything there is a season,
A time for every purpose under heaven.
ECCLESIASTES 3:1 NKJV

We have all heard it from more seasoned moms: "Enjoy your time now; children grow fast." It seems they are eager to give younger moms a piece of advice attained over the years. Perhaps it was the same advice they were given. If we read between the lines, though, we can see that it isn't advice they are trying to give; rather, it's the gift of perspective.

For a mother, the days can be excruciatingly long, but the years fly by. When we are surviving the younger years, it feels like the evening will never come. The clock seems to get slower during the afternoon. But, the opposite can be said when our children get older. The clock seems to speed up, and we can't get enough time with our young adults. We then realize how very quickly they will leave our homes.

Do you find yourself wondering why you wished away those younger years of messes and diapers? Don't miss your current season by always looking to the next one. The gift of perspective knows that there were treasures in the young seasons as well.

Integrity

Let integrity and uprightness preserve me,
For I wait for You.
PSALM 25:21 NKJV

Having integrity means we lack nothing and live without imperfection. It sounds impossible. But in Christ, we are made whole and complete— free from any blemish and stain. Therefore, integrity is present in every believer.

The good news is it's not something we have to search for or summon up. We are able to live in integrity and make choices according to his will because of the work that God has already done in us. Our integrity is compromised only when we choose to walk out of his wholeness.

In what ways do you choose to walk away from his wholeness?
In what ways do you demonstrate integrity?

Tattletale

"Why worry about a speck in your friend's eye when you have a log in your own? How can you think of saying to your friend, 'Let me help you get rid of that speck in your eye,' when you can't see past the log in your own eye?"

MATTHEW 7:3-4 NLT

Where there are children, there will be tattling. Just about every child ends up on both sides of this issue in the first decade of life. For some, the urge to out wrongdoers becomes powerful, and a tattletale is born.

Tattletales who make it to adulthood without outgrowing their penchant for sharing the flaws and foibles of others get a new name: Gossip. We've all heard the expression, "Nobody likes a tattletale," but have you ever wondered where it came from? What's wrong with exposing wrongdoing? In his incredible Sermon on the Mount, Jesus both originated the complaint against tattletales and exposed the reason: drawing attention to the flaws of others takes the focus off our own.

Can you ask God to show you any logs you may be overlooking in your life? Thank him for trusting you with this important parenting lesson when you need to help your children learn to worry about themselves.

February

Love takes no pleasure in evil
but rejoices over the truth.
Love patiently accepts all things.
It always trusts, always hopes, and always endures.
Love never ends.

1 Corinthians 13:6-8 NCV

Lasting Peace

"Peace I leave with you; my peace I give you.
I do not give to you as the world gives.
Do not let your hearts be troubled and do not be afraid."

JOHN 14:27 NIV

We often think of peace as a temporary emotion. Perhaps when everything in our world is right, we can be at peace. However, the peace that is given to us is more than a feeling; rather, a sense of security that lives in us every day, all day.

Peace gives us the ability to stay strong even when life is hard. Peace comforts us when our world falls apart. God's peace drives fear from our hearts. As his children, we can let go of our worries. We can claim peace in our hearts and in our children's as well.

Do you or your children struggle with anxiety?
Take God's peace that belongs to you. And be free.

Winter Blues

That my soul may sing praise to You and not be silent.
O LORD my God, I will give thanks to You forever.
PSALM 30:12 NASB

A number of mothers find themselves stuck in long winters. They envision Floridians lying outside applying sunscreen to their toasty skin. They think if only they could be somewhere warm, they would be happy. But, the Floridians think about those who live in cooler states in the summer. As they endure day after day of 100+ degree temperatures and impossible humidity, they find themselves longing for a 70-degree summer day where the heat doesn't make them or their children nauseated.

It's easy to think contentment will come from a particular place. If it isn't the weather that has us down, it's our house, our job, our weight. This is because contentment was never meant to come from places or things. It comes from being close to him and walking in gratitude.

Can you see how complaint creeps into your life and takes over your mood? Try thanking God for your blessings today and see what happens.

Mom Fail

*"Can you pick grapes from thornbushes, or figs from thistles?
A good tree produces good fruit, and a bad tree produces bad fruit.
A good tree can't produce bad fruit,
and a bad tree can't produce good fruit."*
MATTHEW 7:16-18 NLT

Maybe not today, but one day, you will wonder whether you have failed as a mother. This most important mission of your life—to raise a loving, caring, responsible human being and send them into the world to share God's light—will seem like a task you are simply not up to.

This feeling may last a short time, as a child goes through a phase of selfishness or ungratefulness, or it may take a much longer road as we watch our sweet baby struggle with addiction or a life of crime. We can be reassured by Jesus' words. If we are good, only good fruit can come from our lives regardless of how things may appear.

Do you love God with all your heart? Have you accepted the free gift of salvation through the sacrifice of Jesus? Rest assured. You are doing this mothering thing right. Cling to God's promises and savor his Word.

Seeking Boldly

When one turns to the Lord, the veil is removed. Now the Lord is the Spirit, and where the Spirit of the Lord is, there is freedom. And we all, with unveiled face, beholding the glory of the Lord, are being transformed into the same image from one degree of glory to another. For this comes from the Lord who is the Spirit.

2 CORINTHIANS 3:16-18 ESV

How wonderful it is that God made a way for us to see his glory and all of its fullness. We mothers can go freely to him without hesitation. We have permission to seek him boldly and discover his heart. In that we will be changed.

It is impossible to see God, and know him, and not be changed. The change he produces in us will be a blessing to our children. We can love more like he loves and give grace and mercy like he does. Our parenting style will be transformed to reflect the goodness of who he is.

Do you seek God with all of your heart? Do you understand the freedom you have to know him fully? Never stop seeking him boldly, knowing his heart is vital to being a good mother. What a privilege that your heart will be softened when you know God in such a powerful and intimate way.

Other Adults

The things you have heard me say in the presence of many witnesses entrust to reliable people who will also be qualified to teach others.
2 TIMOTHY 2:2 NIV

You need some friends in your life who love you and your kids: friends who will be committed to your kids almost as much as you are. Other adult relationships are important for your children's maturity, spiritual growth, and understanding of accountability. If your children are struggling with something, and aren't comfortable talking to you about it, you want a mentor that they can talk to that you are both comfortable with.

Some of us may already have those people in our lives. Talking with them about their important role in our children's lives is critical. They can be wise sounding boards in the life of our children if they know what we're expecting.

Who are the people in your life that you know are committed to your kids? Pray with them about what it might look like to have them be more active in the role of giving your children Godly counsel.

My Salvation

Restore to me the joy of Your salvation,
And uphold me by Your generous Spirit.
PSALM 51:12 NKJV

Do we ever stop and enjoy the God of our salvation? We might be involved in many religious activities. We might be in church every week or three times a week. We might have read every popular Bible study out there. We might have attended every conference that has come to our city and regretted the ones we missed. But do we leave these activities feeling full? Maybe it's time to steal away and just enjoy Jesus.

We should take a moment to remember his kindness that drew us to him in the first place. It was his quick forgiveness that let us know that our sins would not be counted against us. We needn't be weighed down by guilt. Jesus bore it all, including our shame, on the cross.

If you never did another thing for God, would that be ok? You aren't getting into heaven based on your merit. You weren't saved based on your good works. You were saved because Jesus did what you were powerless to do. May the Lord refresh you and encourage you today as you delight in him.

The Flock

You are the body of Christ,
and each one of you is a part of it.
1 CORINTHIANS 12:27 NIV

When God created Adam, he also made him a partner. He said it's not good for us to be alone. We are meant to live in fellowship with others. In the Bible we are called sheep, and sheep are apparently very social animals. Sheep require other sheep to be around or they won't display normal sheep-like behavior. They just don't do well on their own.

In light of this, isn't it interesting that we are compared to sheep in Scripture? A sense of normalcy is possible when we don't isolate ourselves from others. There's no need to feel anxious or alone in this journey of life because God has given us a family—his family.

Do you have a flock of sheep to accompany you in this life?
Be encouraged today to embrace the church community around you.
Make the effort to be hospitable and spend dedicated time with others
who are like-minded. You might be surprised just how normal you are.

Sharpening Character

"I have swept away your fences like a cloud,
your sins like the morning mist.
Return to me,
for I have redeemed you."
ISAIAH 44:22 NIV

If anything can reveal our shortcomings and mistakes, motherhood can. It's a hard job! It tests our patience, our faithfulness, and our ability to give unselfishly and joyfully. It completely stretches our character in ways it has never been stretched before.

Motherhood sheds light on our weaknesses and keeps us humble. God uses our children to unearth our weaknesses and encourage change.

How have your children sharpened your character? Have you ever ended a terrible day feeling awful, knowing that you have let your children and God down? Be encouraged in those moments because he gives you grace. Every day is a new day.

Age to Come

"He will wipe every tear from their eyes,
and there will be no more death or sorrow or crying or pain.
All these things are gone forever."

REVELATION 21:4 NLT

God wants us to be encouraged by the Age to Come. He is fully aware of the heaps of sorrows and trials in this life. He is aware not only because he knows us fully and knows the burdens that we bear, but also because he walked this earth and felt the heartaches and temptations that abound. Because of this, he has gone to great lengths to give us everything we need to remain encouraged and sustained while we are here on earth.

God knows that our hope is ignited when he gives us glimpses of heaven. He wants us to know what it will look like. He wants us to know that he longs for us to come to him. He wants us to know that he is preparing our rooms even now.

Do your sorrow and trials feel like they are consuming you?
God knows that as you look past your momentary afflictions,
your heart will be encouraged by his promises of the Age to Come.

Let God Win

Be alert and of sober mind.
Your enemy the devil prowls around like a roaring lion
looking for someone to devour.
1 PETER 5:8 NIV

Don't believe the lies. There is an enemy out there who wants to steal, kill, and destroy. One of the most powerful ways he does that is through filling our hearts with things we think are true about ourselves. Those lies fill our minds with hatred, so that when we look in the mirror, we start hating what we see. "I'm so ugly and fat." "I don't deserve anything good in my life." "I screwed up again; why do I even try?"

These thoughts make the Father who created us weep. Beloved daughters, he loves us! He knits us together and sets us apart. He cherishes every breath we take, and in the name of Jesus we can rebuke the enemy so those lies no longer fill our heads and overtake our hearts. When we walk in the lies that we are unloved, ugly, or undeserving, the enemy wins.

What are the lies that tear you down? Ask Jesus to lift the veil from your eyes so you can see clearly. The truth is that you serve a God who would move mountains for you, a Father who loves his daughter more than anything else and delights in seeing her smile, and a Creator who made you like no other.

Happiness or Joy

*"Now is your time of grief,
but I will see you again and you will rejoice,
and no one will take away your joy."*
JOHN 16:22 NIV

The pursuit of happiness is in the center of western culture. We often seek it in materialism and experiences. However, happiness is only a quick band-aid that masks our pain and sorrow. In time, happiness fades and the hollow spot that joy should fill remains. And so the search continues. We find ourselves stuck in a continual cycle of filling the emptiness with temporary happiness.

True joy, however, is rooted deep in a believer's heart, fueled only by the confidence that is Jesus Christ. Unlike happy feelings, joy is not an emotion that easily comes and goes based on present circumstances. Joy remains firmly rooted despite trials and tribulations.

Are you pursuing happiness or joy? Joy is an affirmation of your complete trust in Jesus and a result of being thankful for what he has done.

love the Joneses

*"'Love the Lord your God with all your heart and with all your soul
and with all your mind and with all your strength.'
The second is this: 'Love your neighbor as yourself.'
There is no commandment greater than these."*
MARK 12:30-31 NIV

When God commanded us to love our neighbors as ourselves, he wasn't saying to have them over for dinner one night and check it off our list. We should love them literally as we love ourselves and our children. This can be difficult. We can't get over that unkind comment made last week, or last year.

We are commanded to love even when it doesn't come naturally to us. Our flesh wants to seek revenge or simply not be hospitable. Jesus loved all he encountered. He desires us to be his hands and feet: his walking-and-talking love here on earth. When we say that we love the Lord, and yet do not show it to those around us, we look no different than the world.

Who is that person or family you've wanted to connect with but haven't? Can you invite them to coffee or over for dinner sometime? You can spread the love of Jesus by loving those around you—by engaging in conversation, inviting them into your home, or learning about their life.

Effective Discipling

"Let the little children come to me, and do not hinder them,
for the kingdom of God belongs to such as these."
LUKE 18:16 NIV

We know that children loved to be around Jesus because he loved to be around them. Children are perceptive. They wouldn't keep going to someone if that person didn't like them. Jesus' love toward them was deeply compelling.

As mothers, our most important job is to point our children to Jesus. Churches and ministries provide many aids to assist us in our job of discipling our children, but we must make sure the fruit of these aids is drawing our children closer to God and not hindering their growth. While many of these tools and programs might be helpful, they can never replace a child's own parent sitting down with them and pointing them to the Lord.

Do you spend time discipling your children or do you let other ministries do it? You will care far more about your child's spiritual growth than a volunteer will, and you will be better able to detect if the program is helping your child really know God. Do your best to make sure your children view God rightly.

Unfailing Love

I am convinced that nothing can ever separate us from God's love. Neither death nor life, neither angels nor demons, neither our fears for today nor our worries about tomorrow—not even the powers of hell can separate us from God's love. No power in the sky above or in the earth below—indeed, nothing in all creation will ever be able to separate us from the love of God that is revealed in Christ Jesus our Lord.

ROMANS 8:38-39 NLT

Could your child lose your love? Think of the worst things they've ever done, or if they are still very young, imagine the worst they could do. Now picture them sleeping. Recall the day they were born. Despite any level of anger, disappointment, or betrayal, could you honestly turn off your love for them?

Now let's think on this: God loves us more.

Consider all the evidence in your life of God's love for you. Write out a prayer of thanksgiving and love to the one who loves you without condition and without fail.

Heirlooms

"I will establish my covenant as an everlasting covenant between me and you and your descendants after you for the generations to come, to be your God and the God of your descendants after you."
GENESIS 17:7 NIV

An heirloom is something of great value passed down from generation to generation. Mothers can give their daughters and sons the most precious heirlooms to treasure and pass on to their own children: an heirloom that is more precious than diamonds and rings—an heirloom of faith.

We should purpose to live our lives with complete trust in God. Our confidence in him is a wonderful testimony to our children of his faithfulness. We can live out a life of faith before them.

What spiritual heirlooms are you passing on to your children?
Let them see your head bowed and arms raised in worship to
Jesus Christ. Then they will remember your life devoted to God
and will share it with their children and grandchildren.
They will own the faith that you possessed.

Value in the Menial

"I have given you an example to follow.
Do as I have done to you."
JOHN 13:15 NLT

The tasks of motherhood can sometimes take on an oppressive quality. As intelligent, vibrant beings, full of life and promise and acquiring wisdom every day, mothers can begin to feel underutilized, underappreciated, and overwhelmed.

When this happens, take a look at Jesus and what he showed his disciples. His last task—his final act of service—was to pick up a towel, get down on his knees, and wash their feet. Tenderly, lovingly, he took each disciple's foot into his hands, removed the grime, and soothed the blisters and calluses. It was a lowly job, and it demonstrated the highest love. This is how precious you are to me, his simple act said.

Can you allow this verse to help you begin to see the more menial, thankless aspects of your role in a new way? Do you believe you are following Jesus' example when you wipe runny noses, change dirty diapers, or even pick up discarded juice boxes and soda cans? Why, or why not?

Like a Child

Then Jesus called for the children and said to the disciples,
"Let the children come to me. Don't stop them!
For the Kingdom of God belongs to those who are like these children."
LUKE 18:16 NLT

Children who know they are loved by their father don't approach him with fear. It is so sweet to see little ones run into their father's arms with abandon. They know without a doubt that his arms will receive them and hold them close. They don't question their father's love for them. They expect to be received and carried.

Is this how we approach God: like a child who knows she is loved? Or do we forget how loved we are and fear him for where we have fallen short? Do we let our guilt hinder us from running into the Father's arms?

How do you approach God? He desires you to run to him. He bids you to come like a little child. He will always receive you with open arms.

Delayed Results

*"The seed on good soil stands for those with a noble and good heart,
who hear the word, retain it, and by persevering produce a crop."*
LUKE 8:15 NIV

Mothering day in and day out can get wearisome. Life in general can get wearisome. It can be repetitive and monotonous. Many times we don't see any direct benefit from our labor. If we have young children, we might not see growth or even sprouts from seeds we've planted for years to come. Because of this, it is easy to get weary and wonder if what we're doing is fruitful work.

Daughters, don't grow weary. Weariness seems to be the direct result of delayed results. We wouldn't grow weary if we immediately saw all the effects of our labor. But when we are sowing seeds in little hearts, it takes time to see the fruit.

Do you feel like your work is fruitful? Ask God for the gift of perspective.
Remember, you are in this for the long haul. Be patient and faithful.
In due time, you will reap a harvest if you don't give up.

Expectations

Know that wisdom is such to your soul;
if you find it, there will be a future,
and your hope will not be cut off.
PROVERBS 24:14 ESV

How many mothers have dropped their children off in the nursery at church and left them crying? Not wanting to release their grip on safety, the children cling to their mothers like newborn kittens, claws out and not letting go. Moms start whispering to them that they will be fine, that mommy will be back, that they will have fun with their friends. Somewhat reluctantly, they hand them over to the childcare volunteer with an apologetic look and quickly back out of the room. It can be a devastating feeling.

The morning they envisioned of sitting and gleaning wisdom from the sermon has vanished. Instead, they stare at the screen wondering if their child's number will be called. They're distracted from fully enjoying the morning they had expected. Expectations. Our expectations can let us down in unthinkable ways. They can take us away from enjoying the moment and are often too controlling.

How do expectations sometimes hinder your experience? Every once in a while, practice the art of giving up your expectation to God. It is out of your hands and rests in the hands of the Father who knows best.

Supernatural Patience

The Holy Spirit produces this kind of fruit in our lives: love, joy, peace, patience, kindness, goodness, faithfulness, gentleness, and self-control.
GALATIANS 5:22-23 NLT

Jesus expects supernatural patience. Give them both cheeks to slap. Give them your shirt and your coat. If they force you to walk one mile, go two. Give to anyone who asks, he tells us in Matthew 5:39-42. Holding ourselves up to this standard, especially as mothers, can make even the most patient moms feel like failures.

Who hasn't lost it when met with disrespect and ingratitude? What do we do? How do we become patient, especially if it's not in our nature? The short answer: we don't. Jesus knows us. He knows this mothering business is hard! Supernatural patience requires supernatural help, and that's why he gives us the Holy Spirit.

Think of a recent occurrence where you struggled with—and lost—your patience. What were the triggers? What was the outcome? How did you feel afterward? Lean on the assurance of Galatians 5:22-23 and invite the Spirit to take that burden from you.

Delete

To the praise of the glory of His grace, which He freely bestowed on us in the Beloved. In Him we have redemption through His blood, the forgiveness of our trespasses, according to the riches of His grace which He lavished on us.

EPHESIANS 1:6-8 NASB

Immediately after the moment, we want to hit delete. We want to go back in time just a few minutes when we could feel our blood pressure rising and knew we might say something we'd regret. We knew we might lose control because we just couldn't handle it anymore. We were done.

But the moment comes, we react, and then we apologize: it's the vicious cycle of our humanness. Thankfully, through the blood of Jesus Christ and our repentance, we are forgiven, set free, and released from the burden of our mistakes. We are given a clean slate to start over. Some days that gift feels bigger than other days. Some days, as moms, we rely, heavily, on the grace of our Lord and Savior just to get through the day. And that is okay.

Have you wanted to hit delete recently? Do you know you are forgiven through the blood of Jesus? Accept his gift; you are forgiven. Forgive yourself and keep moving forward.

Admitting Fault

If we claim we have no sin, we are only fooling ourselves and not living in the truth. But if we confess our sins to him, he is faithful and just to forgive us our sins and to cleanse us from all wickedness. If we claim we have not sinned, we are calling God a liar and showing that his word has no place in our hearts.

1 John 1:8-10 NLT

Depending on how old your children are, they may not know yet that you are not perfect. If you are still in that honeymoon phase of motherhood, enjoy it; it will be over soon enough.

Because we are all sinners, our kids will see us sin. Because of their proximity and the intimacy of the relationship, they'll see it a lot. Let them see! Admitting our faults and failures is one of the best ways we can teach them about God's grace. Let them know God forgives us the moment we regret and confess our actions.

Do you struggle with letting your children see your vulnerable, less-than-perfect side? Or have trouble admitting when you are in the wrong? Ask God to help you examine your heart, and to bless you with the freedom and confidence to admit your shortcomings—to him, to your children, and to yourself. Thank him for loving you just as you are.

Jesus Intercedes

He is able, once and forever, to save those who come to God through him. He lives forever to intercede with God on their behalf.

HEBREWS 7:25 NLT

Do you know that Jesus loves to pray? Praying wasn't a burdensome discipline to Jesus when he walked the earth. He didn't do it because he was told to. He didn't do it because he was trying to fill some quota of time that his local synagogue leader told him needed to be filled. He prayed because he wanted to. He prayed because he knew he had a dad that wanted to hear him.

Jesus prayed for many things when he was on earth. He prayed for his disciples that were before him, but he also prayed for us. What's beautiful is that Jesus is still praying. He is currently sitting nice and close to his Father, and he is talking.

Can you fathom that Jesus is praying for you? He knows the intricacies of your heart better than you do. He is asking his Father to strengthen and encourage you. If you have ever wondered if anyone out there is praying for you, put that thought to rest. Your wonderful Savior lives continually to make intercession for you.

Would He

Trust in the LORD with all your heart;
do not depend on your own understanding.
Seek his will in all you do,
and he will show you which path to take.
PROVERBS 3:5-6 NLT

What would Jesus do? The expression may have become a cliché, but the question is the most important one we can teach our children to ask themselves. It only takes a few seconds, but those seconds could change the entire course of their lives.

Would Jesus stand up for the girl being teased? Would Jesus lie about where he was going? Would he take that drink? This world offers endless temptations, and some of it can be a lot of fun—at least in the moment. Whether it's us, a trusted friend, or an intriguing new acquaintance, most children want the opinion of someone for just about every decision they make. Lead them to consult the only source that matters: encourage them to pray!

This isn't just an issue for children is it? Moms can easily get caught up in the moment too. God's wisdom is the only true wisdom. Open your heart to God; let him show you the parts you are keeping from him, the decisions you save for yourself. Ask him for the courage to turn everything over to him.

Time for Celebration

"The LORD your God is in your midst,
A victorious warrior.
He will exult over you with joy,
He will be quiet in His love,
He will rejoice over you with shouts of joy."
ZEPHANIAH 3:17 NASB

Birthday cake, colorful balloons, banners, and joyfully wrapped gifts... celebrating our children's birthdays is a wonderful and timeless tradition. We take extra care to make sure that the birthday girl or boy feels loved, treasured, and valuable. Birthdays are an opportunity to celebrate another year with our sweet children. We ponder their wonderful place and presence in our family.

We are not the only ones who enjoy celebrating our children. It warms God's heart to celebrate them as well. He was the one that created them with so much thought, care, and detail. Each day in our children's lives has value and importance to the Father. To him, every day is worth being celebrated.

Do you know how loved and celebrated you are by God?
The way you celebrate your children is the way the Lord loves
to celebrate you—every single day. He loves to love you.

Called to Rest

The LORD is like a father to his children,
tender and compassionate to those who fear him.
For he knows how weak we are;
he remembers we are only dust.
PSALM 103:13-14 NLT

One of the most effective things we can do in a day is rest. As moms, our time is pulled in multiple directions constantly, and we are regularly meeting others' needs. God knows, and he masterfully designed you to need rest. If a vehicle has a problem, one of the best people to take the car to would be the engineers who created it. Why? Because they would know every intimate part of the vehicle, and they would quickly be able to diagnose the problem.

God is humankind's designer. If anyone can diagnose our ailments, it's God. And throughout Scripture, he calls us to rest.

Can you take time to rest today? God knows that you aren't a machine and you weren't meant to run continually. He designed you to stop and recharge. It isn't weakness that makes you tired; it's his design. Tired mom, don't fight him on it. Stop and rest.

Surrounded by Suffering

You keep track of all my sorrows.
You have collected all my tears in your bottle.
You have recorded each one in your book.
PSALM 56:8 NLT

Suffering surrounds us. The orphan is scared and hungry; the widow cries at night, her pillow soaked with pain and tears. The mother paces the hospital as her child struggles for breath. The abused hides her scars and braces herself for more. We can't hide from the pain and affliction this world brutally hands out. It is easy to wonder where God is in the midst of all of this suffering.

But we can be confident that he battles without ceasing for the orphan, the widow, the mother, and the abused. We can be assured that he battles with us. We are not alone in our suffering. We are not alone in our pain.

In your suffering, do you feel alone, or are you comforted by the presence of God? He feels with you. He keeps track of all your sorrows. He knows every tear that you shed.

A Call to Sinners

When Jesus heard this, he said,
"Healthy people don't need a doctor—sick people do."
Then he added, "Now go and learn the meaning of this Scripture:
'I want you to show mercy, not offer sacrifices.'
For I have come to call not those who think they are righteous,
but those who know they are sinners."

MATTHEW 9:12-13 NLT

Those unfamiliar with the ins and outs of his ministry might be surprised to learn Jesus spent a lot of time with sinners. Technically, he spent all his time on earth with sinners, since all humans are such. But Jesus actively sought out those considered to be the worst: tax collectors, prostitutes, and others society had written off as unsavory.

Religious leaders were appalled and confused by this. Why would Jesus waste his time on such lost causes, on people who cared little or nothing for the Law?

The next time you find yourself wondering if you are good enough for Jesus, or deserving of his unconditional love, remember this: he came for you. Flawed, hopeless sinner that you are, he came for you. Share with God how this truth makes you feel, then share it with your children.

March

Let us run with endurance the race that is set before us,
looking to Jesus, the founder and perfecter of our faith, who
for the joy that was set before him endured the cross.

HEBREWS 12:1-2 ESV

Corporate Gathering

Let us consider one another in order to stir up love and good works,
not forsaking the assembling of ourselves together,
as is the manner of some, but exhorting one another,
and so much the more as you see the Day approaching.
HEBREWS 10:24-25 NKJV

Sometimes getting to church is hard. The idea of spending a Sunday morning at home on the couch in our pajamas is tempting especially when it has been a long week. The work it would take to get ourselves and others ready to go and out the door is maybe more energy than we have at that moment. Perhaps we feel like going to church is a waste of time when there is so much catching up to do at home: the lawn needs to be mowed or the kitchen needs a deep clean.

Is church worth the effort and the time? Always. Worshiping with fellow believers is refreshing. There is strength that comes from being surrounded by the body of Christ. At church we can receive prayer, encouragement, and comfort in knowing that we are not alone. Church is a place we can find rest and feel at home. We are united with family, receiving a greater understanding of who God is.

Do you find it hard to make it to church consistently? Even when your body is tired, your soul will feel renewed. When your schedule is hectic, you can experience peace. It is definitely worth the effort.

Waiting

Humble yourselves under the mighty power of God,
and at the right time he will lift you up in honor.
Give all your worries and cares to God,
for he cares about you.
1 PETER 5:6-7 NLT

There's a lot of waiting involved in motherhood. We wait for the first smile, first tooth, first steps…then before we know it, we are waiting for them to cross the stage and get their diplomas. In between? More waiting.

It can be difficult sometimes: waiting for the rest of the world to see the potential or pizazz we know is there or waiting for the sound of tires in the driveway long after curfew. Know that God sees it all; he's simply waiting for the right time to execute his plan.

As a mother, what are you waiting for right now? Share your feelings with God. Whether worry, impatience, or even fear, let him comfort you with peace, and assure you he's got it all under control.

Easy Yoke

"My yoke is easy."
MATTHEW 11:30 ESV

Jesus said his yoke is easy. He shared these words with his disciples 2000-plus years ago. They knew exactly what he meant because a yoke was regularly used by many of them. But as time has gone on, yokes aren't exactly an everyday household item. Sometimes we need to do a little study on what Jesus' intended meaning was, so we can enjoy his life-giving words.

Animals that worked side by side were linked with a wooden yoke. This yoke was laid across their necks and kept them together. When two animals were linked like this, they were capable of doing much more than what either could do alone. Furthermore, often a weaker or younger animal was linked to a stronger one. This allowed the stronger one to lead the younger and bear more of the weight.

Do you feel the weight of responsibility driving you down? When Jesus tells you that his yoke is easy, he is inviting you to enjoy his strength and leadership. While he is calling you to service and work, he will bear the majority of the weight. You only have to walk alongside him.

Struggles

*You know that the testing of your faith
produces perseverance.*

JAMES 1:3 NIV

A child is sick. The furnace breaks. You're on your last dollar. A deadline is looming. A loved one passes away. Walking with God does not eliminate us from life's everyday trials. All of these things test our faith. They cause us to question God and his sanctity.

Instead of giving in to despair, we can be thankful in the midst of these things because they cause us to press deeper into the Lord. They reveal our need for him. Our faith in God and our hope in him make us unbreakable when presented with affliction. Trials make us more aware of his work in our lives.

Do the trials in your life control you? When you understand that God prevails over every situation, your faith will be strengthened. Struggles encourage strengthening in the weakest areas of your life.

Those Days

Never stop praying.
1 THESSALONIANS 5:17 NLT

Sometimes by 8:30 a.m. it is easy to feel done. Even though we might have woken up not too long ago, we're tired. Even though we slept eight hours, we're exhausted. We feel sorry for ourselves because of the long day we see before us. Everyone else seemed to wake up on the wrong side of the bed—the very, very wrong side. We wish we could start over. We find ourselves saying to our kids, "We are not having this kind of day," hoping a definitive statement like that will correct their behavior.

This is when our communion with God can turn us around, change our perspective. It reminds us that this life is the beautiful adventure God gave us. He chose us for this role, to these particular children, knowing we were going to have those kind of days. Sometimes he just wants us to sit, put our hearts at the foot of his cross, and let his peace wash over us.

When do you steal away to spend time with God? Do it even if you have to escape to the bathroom. Whisper to him in the shower. Sing shouts of praise in the car. Find moments to look at your life and realize that you are abundantly blessed, even when you want to be done by 8:30 a.m.

Fitting In

The king was distressed,
but because of his oaths and his dinner guests,
he ordered that her request be granted
and had John beheaded in the prison.
MATTHEW 14:9-10 NIV

Has your child ever done something you know they wouldn't normally do in order to fit in or appear a certain way around their friends? Depending on their age, witnessing this may be a daily occurrence in your life, which is painful to watch.

One of the most startling examples in the Bible of this human desire to save face comes from King Herod. Following a performance by his stepdaughter at a banquet for many of his friends, Herod promised her anything she wished. He mother persuaded her to ask for the head of John the Baptist (who had offended her by criticizing her marriage to the king) on a platter. Herod knew he shouldn't agree, but he couldn't bear to be seen as a coward or have his promises counted as unreliable in front of his guests.

At what age do we become slaves to the opinions of others? Clearly, ordering a violent death is an extreme example, but the lesson is universal. Spend some time with God asking him to reveal weaknesses in your heart. Ask him to help you teach your children to cling to God over the need to fit in.

Heart Center

Brothers and sisters, think about the things that are good and worthy of praise. Think about the things that are true and honorable and right and pure and beautiful and respected.

PHILIPPIANS 4:8 NCV

We've said it to our kids on a number of occasions: "You have two choices." Then we proceed to give them their options. Probably one of the choices would be better, but we give them two options to ensure we have a back-up. God also gives us choices. Because of free will, we choose how we spend our time, what we invest our energy in, and what we fill our hearts and minds with.

His desire for us is that we choose him. He wants us to stay in communication with him as we are faced with daily choices. We keep God as our focal point and continually meet him back at our center, so we don't ever steer too far off course.

Where do you choose to spend the majority of your time?
What choices could you eliminate to stay centered on Jesus?
In a busy life of choices, it's important to know your back-up is also your best option: seeking God and choosing life with him.

New Mercies

The faithful love of the LORD never ends!
His mercies never cease.
Great is his faithfulness;
his mercies begin afresh each morning.
LAMENTATIONS 3:22-23 NLT

Did you have a hard day yesterday? Perhaps a hard week? Better yet, are you just in a difficult season? Nothing tests us like mothering. It exposes our weaknesses and sins better than any other role. Be encouraged, dear daughters, we aren't alone. Life isn't easy for anyone. We are all called to take up our cross and follow Jesus.

God doesn't want us to feel defeated though. He wants us to know his infinite and powerful grace. Where we are weak, he is strong. He has new mercy for us each day. Yes, that's right! We may have used up our allotment of mercy yesterday, but there is new mercy available for us today. Every morning, he pours fresh mercy into our hearts. He knows we need it.

Do you feel like you ask for mercy too often?
Today, you can receive all the mercy you need from him. He won't remind you of the mercy you used yesterday. In fact, he expected you to use it. That is precisely why he gives you fresh mercy today.

Body of Christ

Speaking the truth in love, we are to grow up in every way into him who is the head, into Christ, from whom the whole body, joined and held together by every joint with which it is equipped, when each part is working properly, makes the body grow so that it builds itself up in love.
EPHESIANS 4:15-16 ESV

Looking back in your life, can you name the individuals who were a huge part of your walk with God and your testimony? Can you count the people that have been dear to you, who either shared the gospel with you, or loved and cared for you deeply? Souls who have supported and served alongside you? Friendships that have pointed you toward Christ?

Those people are precious gifts. God blesses us with incredible people to do life with. The body of Christ is a wonderful thing. We don't ever have to be alone.

Do you know that in Christ, you are adopted into a huge, amazing family. Take account of the people God has placed in your life and thank him for them.

Being Known

You discern my going out and my lying down;
you are familiar with all my ways.
Before a word is on my tongue,
you, LORD, know it completely.
You hem me in behind and before,
and you lay your hand upon me.
PSALM 139:3-5 NIV

When you ask a brand-new mother how things are going, you often hear something like, "It's great; we just loving getting to know him," or "She's wonderful; we're having so much fun figuring out who she is!"

It's amazing, isn't it, that within the first days of life these little people already have an identity? One loves to be swaddled, and the other can't relax unless kicking legs and waving arms. For the rest of our lives we have the privilege of getting to know them. Still more amazing is that God already knows everything about them and about us.

Do you love knowing that God knows every move you make, or that he can anticipate your words before you speak them? Perhaps you take joy in knowing he is all around you as you move through the world. Take a few moments to revel in being so completely known.

Value in Planning

Go to the ant, O sluggard;
consider her ways, and be wise.
Without having any chief, officer, or ruler,
she prepares her bread in summer
and gathers her food in harvest.

PROVERBS 6:6-8 ESV

Every mom delights in her children's full and happy bellies. Often we work hard in the kitchen with our families in mind, happily preparing and serving warm and nutritious meals to them. Doing so brings joy. It's no wonder many households tend to gather in the kitchen.

Even though today we are able to conveniently pick up fresh produce and meat from a local grocery store, a lot of forethought goes into each meal served. We carefully manage and budget our finances, often planning meals weeks in advance to ensure that our children don't go hungry. It is a lot of work. However, there is so much wisdom in planning and working ahead. Planting gardens, cutting coupons, planning meals, and stocking our cupboards and freezers can be a huge blessing for our families.

Can you see the value in planning ahead? Do you know how valuable you are to the Lord? God is working through you when you work in your home and in your kitchen. Your family is blessed to have you in it.

Not Abandoned

"The LORD will not abandon His people on account of His great name, because the LORD has been pleased to make you a people for Himself."
1 SAMUEL 12:22 NASB

While we are mothers, do we realize that we also get to be children? God will always call us his children. He enjoys being our dad, and we can enjoy being his child. That means we can still ask him our questions the way a child would. It means we can still tell him that we don't have it all figured out. It means that we don't have to bear the weight of providing for all our children's needs. We can simply ask our Father in heaven to take care of them in the same way he takes care of us.

Children aren't afraid to say when they are frightened, confused, or worried. They are expected to take these needs to their parents and get direction and comfort. We can do the same with God.

Mother, do you know you have an invitation to go to God as a child?
He delights in this because he loves being your Dad.
Can you relate to God fearlessly as a child would?

Voice of Love

"I have given them the glory you gave me,
so they may be one as we are one.
I am in them and you are in me.
May they experience such perfect unity
that the world will know that you sent me
and that you love them as much as you love me."

JOHN 17:22-23 NLT

When we live for other voices, we will quickly become worn out and discouraged. Other people's expectations for how we should live, act, and be are sometimes unreachable. There is one voice that matters, and it can come in a variety of forms—the voice of God.

What God would tell us is that we are loved, we are cherished, and we add significant value. We are his beloved, his daughters, his beautiful creation. This is the voice that matters. This is the voice to come back to when we feel like we're not enough.

What are the voices you typically listen to? Can you ignore them and focus only on the voice that matters? He will encourage you and remind you that you are enough and nothing you do or don't do is going to make him love you any more or any less. Soak it in, so you can drown out all the other voices.

Imperfectly Balanced

"My dear Martha, you are worried and upset over all these details!
There is only one thing worth being concerned about.
Mary has discovered it, and it will not be taken away from her."
Luke 10:41-42 NLT

Getting a scale to balance doesn't necessarily mean both sides are evenly weighted. Isn't that a relief? During this season of your life, the "mom" side of your scale is weighed down—heavily. If you also work outside the home, balance can seem permanently out of reach. Your family is your #1 priority, so something, maybe exercise, maybe cleaning bathrooms, maybe pursuing a long-held dream, is hovering out of sight. It's ok. Until the scale crashes, it's in balance.

As long as we remember to seek the Father's guidance, truth, and wisdom, the scale isn't going to crash. Everything that needs to be done will be done. He's got us. We just have to keep our eyes on what's important. Do you have an achievable idea of balance? If you feel like Martha, always rushing around trying to get it all done, you are not alone. How can you begin sitting at the feet of Jesus and letting him tell you what's important?

What would it take for you to simply enjoy reading another story with your three-year-old without worrying about the un-done dishes? Or studying your Bible without thinking of your to-do list?

Light and Warmth

"You are the light of the world.
A town built on a hill cannot be hidden.
Neither do people light a lamp and put it under a bowl.
Instead they put it on its stand,
and it gives light to everyone in the house."
MATTHEW 5:14-15 NIV

Mothers are a light in their homes. What a privilege it is to give our children Jesus. In everything we do, we should do it for Jesus. Our homes will be warm—a place of refuge for our sweet children—when centered around God. Our children will come to know Jesus through our actions toward them and others. Our character will be a testimony of God's love and grace.

In our homes, our children have the opportunity to grow up knowing and loving Jesus. The world they face is cold and dark, but they will come to know that their homes are a place of security and rest.

What does it mean for you to have a Christ-centered home?
Are you a light in your home?

I Am Struggling

God's will is for you to be holy, so stay away from all sexual sin.
Then each of you will control his own body
and live in holiness and honor—not in lustful passion
like the pagans who do not know God and his ways.

1 THESSALONIANS 4:3-5 NLT

Help! I am struggling too! Has the media age come into your home and plagued you? There have been many teachings and resources developed to protect our children from sinful addictions online. Have we been more diligent with guarding their minds than our own? We aren't alone.

The Bible says sin entangles. Sexual sin seems to get us tangled up fairly quickly. Sometimes it takes a little while to untangle something. It can and will happen with perseverance, but it's imperative that we don't get paralyzed by discouragement.

Can you understand that learning to control your body is a process? Complete victory might not happen overnight. Dear child, take heart that God will cleanse and forgive you every time you come to him. In addition to that, he strengthens your resolve to turn away from sin and run to him.

A New Lens

*Our present troubles are small and won't last very long.
Yet they produce for us a glory that vastly
outweighs them and will last forever!
So we don't look at the troubles we can see now;
rather, we fix our gaze on things that cannot be seen.*
2 CORINTHIANS 4:17-18 NLT

Some mothers might remember the newborn fog: the time when we're barely sleeping and our days and nights blend together into one long week. We're exhausted, smelly from not having time to shower, and maybe feeling a little out of our element. But, once we are out of that phase, we look back on it and wish we could be there again. Suddenly those foggy moments are fond memories. We forget the smelly days, and the early morning feedings feel like a peaceful dream of cuddling our newborns.

Our perspective shifts as time propels us forward. But how do we gain perspective for where we are? We ask God for a new way to look at something. In doing so, he fills us with peace for our situation.

Ask God for a change in perspective about a certain situation.
He can change your heart in a timely moment, so you can appreciate
the season you are in.

No Holding Back

"For I know the plans I have for you," declares the LORD,
"plans to prosper you and not to harm you,
plans to give you hope and a future.
Then you will call on me and come and pray to me,
and I will listen to you.
You will seek me and find me
when you seek me with all your heart."
JEREMIAH 29:11-13 NIV

God wants wonderful things for you. He wants great things for your children. He has blessing upon blessing stored up just waiting for the right time.

Perhaps we are in a season that feels more like punishment. Maybe we have even begun to doubt his intentions toward us as we struggle with a defiant child, an empty bank account, or a serious illness. We have to trust him without holding back. He wants our whole hearts, and he wants them at a time when it might be hard to give them. But if we do, we let his blessings flow.

Whether this is a dark time in your life or one you are certain of his love and provision, can you know the truth of these verses? Place them somewhere you can see or find them easily and read them aloud whenever you begin to doubt.

Transformation

I am certain that God, who began the good work within you, will continue his work until it is finally finished on the day when Christ Jesus returns.
PHILIPPIANS 1:6 NLT

When we give our lives to God, we expect to be radically and completely changed from the inside out. We get frustrated and discouraged when we discover old habits are hard to break, and we keep getting ensnared in the same temptation.

It is tempting to quit. But we should be encouraged! We are new in Christ; his work in us is continual. Sanctification is a process—a very tough and painful one. His grace will cover us and he promises to complete his work. He hasn't left us or abandoned us.

Are you frustrated that you are not the person you want to be?
Take comfort in knowing the Holy Spirit is transforming you today.
Continue to spend time in the Word. Worship God. Love him. By
spending time with him and knowing him, you'll become a new person.
Take delight in his ability to transform you!

Mourning into Dancing

May your unfailing love be my comfort,
according to your promise to your servant.
PSALM 119:76 NIV

Grief can look so different for each person, but it all fits into the same heart-wrenching mold of confusion, anger, sadness, and doubt. More often than not, grief surprises us with an upheaval of all we knew to be solid in life. Trusting in a God who loves us unconditionally gets muddled in those moments. Our solid foundation becomes spongy and uncertain.

Hopefully, with the gentle knocks on our hearts to remember his great love for us, the confusion turns into understanding and sadness into joy for the moments we were able to share. Our spongy, doubt-filled mind will cling to the truth that we knew deep in our souls: that God is good and he has a plan for our lives.

Have you had a moment of grief where you've doubted God's plan for your life? Be assured that he will comfort you and gently turn your heart back to him. You will laugh again in the morning and find peace in your grief.

Led to Repentance

Do you think lightly of the riches of His kindness and tolerance and patience, not knowing that the kindness of God leads you to repentance?

ROMANS 2:4 NASB

Are you discouraged by your child's behavior? Is there continuous rebelling in a certain area? Do you feel like you have tried every discipline under the sun to change them? Perhaps there is another route you can try: the route of kindness.

It is God's kindness that leads us to repentance. Imagine that for a moment. God knows a corrective word spoken in love will produce more than a shouting match. He knows it is his firm but gentle touch, that will bring about a heart change. He is a kind disciplinarian. When we receive and absorb his love, it becomes easier to leave childish ways of sin behind. God knows that we respond much better to kindness than cruelty.

It is important that however you discipline your child, you do it in kindness. Can you ask God to grant you the grace to know the difference as you shape the lives he's put before you?

Covering Prayer

"I'm not asking you to take them out of the world, but to keep them safe from the evil one. They do not belong to this world any more than I do. Make them holy by your truth; teach them your word, which is truth. Just as you sent me into the world, I am sending them into the world."

JOHN 17:15-18 NLT

Jesus' incredible final prayer in the upper room contains his heartfelt requests for his disciples: those present with him at the time and those yet unborn. That's us. Jesus prayed for all who would follow his teaching.

As a mother, it's a prayer worth offering up on behalf of our own children.

Rewrite this prayer and personalize it for your children.
Consider carefully what you are asking of God on their behalf
and thank him for his love and protection.

True Friendship

Confess your sins to each other and pray for each other so that you may be healed. The earnest prayer of a righteous person has great power and produces wonderful results.

JAMES 5:16 NLT

One of the best treasures a mother can have is a close friend: a friend she can fully trust and be open with about her daily struggles and battles. Mothers need a confidant with whom they can be real and transparent on the best days and on the worst. A mother needs a friend who will pray for her, support her, and rejoice with her when she conquers whatever she is struggling with.

Keeping all of our struggles inside is terribly destructive. The enemy wants us to agonize over our temptations and weaknesses alone. He wants us to feel defeated and lost. He wants to destroy us. God wants us to support each other in the messiest parts of our lives, and the only way we can do that is by letting a friend in.

If you struggle with anger, selfishness, or the like, confiding in a friend will bring bright light and healing. Do you have a close friend to share your heart with? Seek her out today.

That Person

*"There is no greater love
than to lay down one's life
for one's friends."*
JOHN 15:13 NLT

Do you have your person? The friend that you go to at two in the morning when you need to talk? Do you have that girlfriend that knows your very worst and loves you for it?

Jesus had a lot of friends in his followers. He told them frequently that he loved them, that they were meant to be his people. He was open and genuine when they disappointed him or when he expected more. He forgave easily. These are all things that we women desire in our relationships. We need to cling to those intimate friends tightly and thank them often.

Are you open enough to let others in on your life? If you're still looking for your two-in-the-morning friend, make sure you're being open and vulnerable with others, and they will likely do the same. It isn't always easy to expose your weakness, but the reward is great.

Need to Breathe

When hard pressed, I cried to the LORD;
he brought me into a spacious place.
PSALM 118:5 NIV

There are days, aren't there, when the walls really do seem to be closing in? Pressed from every side with needs, obligations, expectations, and commitments, you wonder not just how, but if you can keep it all together. Braces, bosses, bills…when do you get to breathe?

The book of Psalms is filled with such pressures, often in the form of angry armies hoping to kill King David. What was his unfailing response? Prayer.

Isn't a spacious place a wonderful image? Take your pressures to the Lord and feel them lift; feel your surroundings and your hope expand. Catch your breath with the one gave you life.

Gentle Discipline

"The LORD disciplines those he loves,
and he punishes each one he accepts as his child."
HEBREWS 12:6 NLT

As mothers, a crucial part of our role is administering discipline. Because of our diverse backgrounds, that word can evoke a range of emotions. Some received discipline from a loving parent, and while not always perfect, they knew they were being disciplined for their good. For others though, discipline might represent cruelty or abuse.

Discipline, as God intends it, is a direct act of love. It is not motivated by a burst of anger or a vengeful heart. Its motivation is for the recipient's own well-being. God disciplines us for our own good using the gentlest means possible to provoke the greatest change. We shouldn't be shocked when our children sin and rebel. It is their nature. But that is also the very reason we cannot let their sin go unnoticed.

Did you know that God calls you to lovingly correct your children so they begin to choose differently? Remember, you aren't hurting them; you are loving them. God disciplines those he loves.

Judge's Seat

He has told you, O man, what is good;
And what does the LORD require of you
But to do justice, to love kindness,
And to walk humbly with your God?

MICAH 6:8 NASB

"She pulled my hair!"

"He took my toy!"

"She won't get out of my room!"

Parenting, whether we like it or not, often puts us in the judge's seat. We are called to train, teach, love, and discipline our children. Our desire is for them to know and love God. It can be completely overwhelming at times and tempting to parent out of anger or frustration. But our children need to be taught the ways of the Lord. They need to know his kindness and mercy. The best way to teach them is to lead by example.

God gives us clear instructions on how to parent: don't favor one child over another, be fair, be a giver of mercy. We all make mistakes and our children are just learning. We need to be humble about our own walk with Jesus.

In what ways can you show your children God's kindness and mercy? Your children don't need a perfect mother, so it won't do them any good pretending you are. Opening up and being apologetic when you make mistakes has such a positive impact on your children's hearts.

Confidence Boost

Do not throw away your confidence; it will be richly rewarded.
You need to persevere so that when you have done the will of God,
you will receive what he has promised.
HEBREWS 10:35-36 NIV

There can be incidents that arise that completely shake our confidence. Where we used to be able to laugh it off, we find ourselves flustered and unsure how to handle the situation. When that happens, insecurities are brought to the surface and sometimes those insecurities hang on for a while.

The enemy loves our insecurities. He loves when we beat ourselves up for little things we might have said, or the way we acted a bit out of character, or how we feel defeated as mothers on that particular day. He loves to see us weighed down with regret. In Hebrews, God tells us to persevere! He does not bow down to the enemy that seeks to destroy us. He does not let him win.

When do you feel the most insecure? Pray about it now and ask God for the confidence to defeat that insecurity. Know God is in your corner shouting praises of encouragement in any and every situation.

Remain in Me

"I am the true vine, and My Father is the vinedresser.
Every branch in Me that does not bear fruit, He takes away;
and every branch that bears fruit,
He prunes it so that it may bear more fruit.
I am the vine, you are the branches;
he who abides in Me and I in him,
he bears much fruit,
for apart from Me you can do nothing."
JOHN 15:1-2, 5 NASB

In John 15, Jesus gives a wonderfully life-giving illustration. He is the vine, God is the vinedresser, and we are the branches. We know that a vinedresser's job is incredibly important. A plant will never bear as much fruit without a vinedresser as it would with one.

God says that the only thing we need to do to bear fruit is to remain in the vine. That is a nice, simple task. If we stay in the vine, he promises to nurture us and sustain us. He also promises to prune us. The pruning isn't for the sake of staying small. It is so we can bear even more fruit.

If you know the vinedresser has your best interest in mind, is it easier to submit yourself willingly to his pruning? All he asks of you is to remain in him. He will do the rest.

Insurance

"I am the resurrection and the life.
The one who believes in me will live,
even though they die;
and whoever lives by believing in me will never die."
JOHN 11:25-26 NIV

These days we have an abundance of insurance at our fingertips. It's bought at a high cost, of course. We have life insurance, car insurance, medical insurance, house insurance. It gives us peace of mind that whatever might happen, we will have security.

Real insurance rests only in the promises of God and our promise of salvation bought by the blood of Jesus Christ. Any other type of insurance pales in comparison. Without God, we will falter no matter how great an insurance plan we own.

Where does your security come from: the insurance plans of the world or the promises of God?

Standing Out

Don't copy the behavior and customs of this world,
but let God transform you into a new person
by changing the way you think.
Then you will learn to know God's will for you,
which is good and pleasing and perfect.
ROMANS 12:2 NLT

Don't you love the fashion statements of little ones? They wear what they love from head to toe with no regard for matching, convention, or trend. Plaid pants under a flowered dress with bunny slippers and a tiara, why not? This phase lasts only a short time, and then even the most confident of children learn to tone it down, to blend in. And we are relieved.

When it comes to their walk with Jesus, we don't want them to fit in at all. We want them to stand out: to always be kind, to refuse gossip, to boldly assert the truth of creation, to unwaveringly choose to save themselves for marriage. It's a tall order. We know this because we struggle with it ourselves. Fitting in feels good; wearing a tiara to Target… not so much.

Have you asked God to transform you? Pour your heart out to him, sharing every aspect of your life you'd like to give up. Ask him to remove your interest in the things you know he doesn't want for you. Share this verse with your children and encourage them do to the same.

April

I have been crucified with Christ.
It is no longer I who live,
but Christ who lives in me.
And the life I now live in the flesh
I live by faith in the Son of God,
who loved me and gave himself for me.

GALATIANS 2:20 ESV

The Credit

As the Scriptures say, "If you want to boast, boast only about the Lord."
When people commend themselves, it doesn't count for much.
The important thing is for the Lord to commend them.
2 CORINTHIANS 10:17-18 NLT

It's tempting, isn't it, to take credit for the amazing people our children are? We feel great when our beautiful daughter is told she looks just like her mom, or someone remarks on our son's gentle patience with younger children saying, "Clearly you are doing something right." And it's true, to a degree.

We have huge influence over our children's lives. But who influences us? Who gave us those pretty cheekbones, and decided we'd be graced with patience and compassion? If our kids are wonderful—if we are wonderful—it's because God wanted it so.

What gifts from God have you passed to your children? How do you feel when those gifts shine? Are you helping them see their specialness as something God wants them to use to further his kingdom?

Shifting Priorities

Offer hospitality to one another without grumbling.
Each of you should use whatever gift you have received to serve others,
as faithful stewards of God's grace in its various forms.
If anyone speaks, they should do so as one who speaks
the very words of God.

1 PETER 4:9-11 NIV

When we become mothers, life naturally changes. And so do the relationships around us. Our friendships tend to shift and take a backseat to the little family we are knitting. We become inwardly involved and focused. It takes a more concentrated effort to pour into our friends. Time is limited, our energy is drained, and our priorities have changed. But good friendships are worth fighting for.

Friends are valuable. Mothering with the support of people that love and care for us is priceless. We need each other.

Consider how you love the people in your life. Do you make time for close friends? Open up your home (even if it is messy), serve and encourage them in the journey, be a shoulder to cry on, or the friend to confide in. Love deeply.

The Busy Bee

The LORD is good to those who depend on him,
to those who search for him.
So it is good to wait quietly
for salvation from the LORD.
And it is good for people to submit at an early age
to the yoke of his discipline:
Let them sit alone in silence
beneath the LORD's demands.
LAMENTATIONS 3:25-28 NLT

We seem to think that the busier we are, the better we are. The more activities our kids are in, the better we are equipping them for whatever is to come. Busyness doesn't mean we are better. But it isn't bad to be busy either as long as we don't have the perspective that the fullness of our lives is determined by how busy we are.

Jesus spent a lot of time in relationship with others. His busy was different than ours. There is so much fullness to be had in quiet evenings at home with your family, a Saturday morning with nothing to do but make pancakes and stay in pajamas, a long walk outside with our kids, or coffee with a friend. Let's not put busy on a pedestal; it has a proper place in life—just not the top rung.

Do you have a full calendar? Slow down. Enjoy the journey.

Confidence in Him

I pray that God, the source of hope,
will fill you completely with joy and peace
because you trust in him.
Then you will overflow with confident hope
through the power of the Holy Spirit.
ROMANS 15:13 NLT

Ever have a day where your confidence seems to have left you? Why did you trust me with these children, God? Don't you know how weak I am, and how scared and small I feel? Even if those days of doubt come more often than not, be confident of this: God knew exactly what he was doing when he trusted you with your precious babies—with his precious babies.

None of us knows what we are doing all the time; every day of every life is something new, except to him. He wrote our stories long ago and wherever we are, whatever we are doing, it's a part of that story. We can give him our love and trust and let him be our strength.

Do you believe God believes in you, and that he will equip you to handle whatever circumstances you face? Share your heart with him, and ask him to fill you with the joy, peace, and confident hope of Romans 15:13.

Rolled Away

*When they looked up, they saw that the stone,
which was very large, had been rolled away.
"You are looking for Jesus the Nazarene, who was crucified.
He has risen! He is not here.
See the place where they laid him."*

MARK 16:4, 6 NIV

Most of us know that Jesus was raised from the dead. Whenever we hear it, we know it to be part of the story of Jesus. But have we ever really meditated on the truth of that statement in the New Testament?

Jesus was raised from the dead! Certainly he can be trusted with our lives. So many times we doubt his love for us. We cast him aside and try to do it all ourselves. We doubt his truth and his healing power. We don't think we can do everything through his strength; yet, in the same breath, we easily accept that Jesus died and rose again. If he can do that, our trials can be overcome in the name of Jesus Christ!

What have you been holding on to that you can trust God with? The stone was rolled away! If you believe that, you can believe that all of his promises are true, and that he loves you enough to care for all the details you are trying to control.

Childlike Humility

"Anyone who becomes as humble as this little child is the greatest in the Kingdom of Heaven. And anyone who welcomes a little child like this on my behalf is welcoming me."

MATTHEW 18:4-5 NLT

Jesus loved kids. He even told his disciples that only those who made themselves childlike would enter the kingdom of heaven. What was it about little children that Jesus found so appealing?

Think about toddlers. How trusting are they? How concerned with the opinions of others? The amusing "me do it" declarations of a two-year-old aside, we rarely meet children who don't recognize their absolute dependence on others.

In what ways do you need to become more childlike?
What lessons could you learn by watching and imitating your kids?
Spend some time with God on this. Ask him to help you help your children retain their humility and trust.

Working with Purpose

*Whatever you do, do well. For when you go to the grave,
there will be no work or planning or knowledge or wisdom.*
ECCLESIASTES 9:10 NLT

Every day you wake up is a new opportunity to put everything you are into your work—whether that work is inside your home or out. You should put your heart and soul into your efforts. You may not like where you are in life, but you were given today, so take advantage of it!

We don't always like the task we are assigned or the jobs that we need to do. Perhaps running after toddlers and changing dirty diapers isn't your dream job. Or maybe you resent sitting in an office and wish you were home. Regardless of where you are and what you do, give it your best.

What opportunities do you have ahead of you today? There is no reward in not trying, but there is joy and a sense of satisfaction in working hard. You do not have to love what you do to give it your all. It may seem pointless and mundane, but it is not.

Serious Business

"If anyone causes one of these little ones—those who believe in me— to stumble, it would be better for them to have a large millstone hung around their neck and to be drowned in the depths of the sea."
MATTHEW 18:6 NIV

Kids learn most of their bad behavior from us. When we see a child in public throwing a tantrum until her bedraggled mother gives in and buys her the object of her desire, we either cringe at the thought of our own children behaving that way, recall a time or times they have, or think, *I can't believe she gave in! No wonder the child acts like that!*

The third response is dangerous if we find ourselves passing judgment, but there is also a crucial lesson embedded in this reaction. We have a God-given responsibility to teach our kids how to behave appropriately. When we reward, encourage, or model wrong behavior, we are essentially causing them to sin. How much do you think this matters to God?

How does this verse affect you? Ask God if you are taking your responsibility to lead your children down the right path as seriously as he requires. Keep in mind his unconditional love and forgiveness as he reveals things to you. Thank him for the mercy of each new day.

Hiding Away

You are my refuge and my shield;
your word is my source of hope.
PSALM 119:114 NLT

How many times have you locked yourself in your room to hide momentarily from the noise, the chaos, and the constant demands of motherhood? It feels good to escape, catch your breath, and regain a measure of sanity.

Hiding is not always an option when you are needed so much. Besides, little ones have a knack for finding you in those moments. Next time motherhood overwhelms you, hide away with God's Word (and perhaps some well-deserved chocolate). He will give you the rest you need. He knows that sometimes all you need is to get away, and he welcomes you.

What aspects of motherhood seem to overwhelm you the most?
God is your escape. In his hiding place he will strengthen you
and renew your hope. Take some time to hide away with the Lord today.

Love Listens

Blessed be the LORD,
Because He has heard the voice of my supplication.
The LORD is my strength and my shield;
My heart trusts in Him, and I am helped;
Therefore my heart exults,
And with my song I shall thank Him.
PSALM 28:6-7 NASB

We love to feel understood. This is particularly true when trouble arises. We don't necessarily want someone to agree with us or make the problem go away, we just want to know that we were heard. When someone shows they are listening, it gives us the gift of love. And when we know we are loved, inevitably our problems seem to shrink.

This principle applies to children as well. If children know they won't get turned away, they'll come to us with a myriad of troubles: their bike broke, their pet frog escaped, or the comb is stuck in their doll's hair. While an adult knows these aren't life-shattering circumstances, a child does not. And that is ok. They aren't meant to be wise adults yet.

How do you feel when someone really listens to you?
Your gift to your child is to genuinely listen to their troubles.
When they know they are loved, their burden becomes light.

Role Models

*"Let your light shine before others,
that they may see your good deeds
and glorify your Father in heaven."*
MATTHEW 5:16 NIV

Children imitate what they see; it's how they learn to operate in this big world. Being a role model is a huge responsibility, and the scary thing is, you are one—all the time—whether you want to be or not. No matter how old or how young, you can be sure of one thing: your kids are watching you. At first, every child wants to be just like Mommy or just like Daddy. Who hasn't caught a little boy or girl with a tool in hand ready to "fix" something, or with lipstick smeared all over their faces?

As time passes, children become more selective about what they adopt. Our optimism and friendliness? Absolutely. Our critical spirit? Not so much. The key to being a good role model is mostly to remember that we are role models. It's how God planned things.

What are you modeling to your children right now? Are they seeing the light you want them to see? How could you shine more brightly today?

Standing Firm

My dear brothers and sisters, stand firm. Let nothing move you.
Always give yourselves fully to the work of the Lord,
because you know that your labor in the Lord is not in vain.

1 CORINTHIANS 15:58 NIV

As mothers, there are countless decisions we make every day. Some decisions are easier than others; we make judgment calls on bedtime, discipline, extracurricular activities, sleepovers, curfews, parties, friends, boyfriends, and the list goes on. There are many grey areas in parenting, and we have to make decisions, clothed in prayer, based on each child.

Then there are the black-and-white decisions: the ones where we clearly know what is right according to God's law. In those times, our decisions may not be favorable or received well by our children. We may feel pressured to bend the rules to keep harmony or to save face, but God calls us to stand firm for him in those moments.

When you are confident of what God's will is, how do you choose to stay firm in your decisions even when your children, or others, plead with you to change your mind? You are parenting for his purpose. Do not bend according to the world.

No Example

We ask God to give you complete knowledge of his will and to give you spiritual wisdom and understanding. Then the way you live will always honor and please the Lord, and your lives will produce every kind of good fruit. All the while, you will grow as you learn to know God better and better.
COLOSSIANS 1:9–10 NLT

Have you no models of godly mothering to look to? Have you asked yourself how it is possible to be a good mother when you yourself lacked one? Sometimes all we can remember are our own mother's faults. We wonder who we can learn from.

We can't underestimate the Lord's power to impart to us all that we need. He is the perfect parent, which means he can give us all the wisdom we need. Know too that those who grew up in "perfect Christian homes" did not have perfect mothers. Every mother fails in some way because she is human. God is ok with that. We all need his help, his forgiveness, and his leadership.

Do you ask God for wisdom before asking others? Inquire of him. You will not be found in want. His promise is to give wisdom generously where it is sought. Take him up on his offer.

The Label Game

Do not love the world or anything in the world. If anyone loves the world, love for the Father is not in them. For everything in the world—the lust of the flesh, the lust of the eyes, and the pride of life—comes not from the Father but from the world. The world and its desires pass away, but whoever does the will of God lives forever.

1 JOHN 2:15-17 NIV

It is so easy to become caught up in a world of stuff: the kind of car we drive, the house we live in, and what schools our kids go to label us as certain people. If we can't achieve those things, we quickly become discouraged and discontent. We feel that life is unfair, and we are somehow below others because we don't have the right stuff.

Jesus tells us something entirely different. He encourages us to set our minds on things that are above (Colossians 3:2). That life he promises us in heaven is the one that matters most.

How have labels affected your life? How can you teach your children not to set their hearts on things of this earth? Do you understand that you matter to God, not your stuff?

Crave the Spirit

Like newborn babies, you must crave pure spiritual milk so that you will grow into a full experience of salvation. Cry out for this nourishment, now that you have had a taste of the Lord's kindness.

1 PETER 2:2-3 NLT

To explain how desperately we should want to know more of God, Peter uses the metaphor of a newborn. Whether you have an infant in your arms right now, or whether those days are many years behind you, close your eyes and go back to that time when the only thing in the world that mattered to your child was to be held in your arms and fed. Think of that angry, purple little face when you took too long to satisfy their hunger, and the almost greedy relief with which they ate once they could.

According to Peter, that is the level of desire—of need—we should bring to our relationship with God.

How would you describe your craving for God: for his Word, his Spirit, his grace? Ask him to open your heart to wanting more and more of him, and less and less of everything else.

Stillness

"Be still, and know that I am God.
I will be exalted among the nations,
I will be exalted in the earth!"
PSALM 46:10 ESV

Be still. Is that phrase even in a mom's vocabulary? The day is short and the to-do list is long. Mothers don't have the luxury of being still unless they are sleeping; even then, their slumber will likely be interrupted.

It is important, though, for moms to quiet themselves before the Lord and be reminded that he is there. God loves us and he cares deeply for us. He wants to be the Lord over our lives.

How can you make room in your day to be still? In the rush and busyness of motherhood, God has not left you alone. He wants to give you rest and encouragement. Quiet times of refreshing for a busy mom's soul are worth seeking out.

Cultivating Love

Love is patient, love is kind.
1 CORINTHIANS 13:4 NASB

Does your love for your children, or one particular child, feel weak? All relationships require tune-ups. They require time and effort. If we don't connect with people on a heart-level, we can't expect to feel deep emotion toward them the moment they walk in the room. We have to intentionally steward our minds and invest quality time into relationships to stir emotion.

If we operate simply as our children's maid, we can start to resent them and their needs. It's important to invest quality time in their lives and find ways to relate to them on their level. Depending on their age, it might require some video game playing, reading the same book 100 times, precariously hiking into their beloved tree house, or watching a sport we care little about. We have to remember that love is kind.

Do you need to spend some extra special time with your children right now? Your love for your child will increase as you step out of your normal duties and play with them. In turn, this will empower you to go back to serving them out of generosity.

Prayers Are Heard

The eyes of the LORD are on the righteous,
and his ears are attentive to their cry.
PSALM 34:15 NIV

Do we know in the depths of our hearts that our prayers are heard: both the shouting cries for help and the gentle whispers of thanksgiving? He knows our every thought before we even think it. This is the Father who created us. This is the Abba that calls us by name. We are his beloved daughters.

Believe it, sweet mothers. We need to let the truth sink into the very deepest parts of our hearts and rest there in thanksgiving. His Word is truth, and he tells us time and time again that he will answer our prayer because we trust in him. Whether through song, action, thought, or speech, he delights in hearing our prayers.

Do you take time daily to pray to your loving Father? If not, start the practice of talking with him in the car, in the shower, or sitting in silence in your room. What you say doesn't have to be fancy or long, God just desires your conversation and communion with him.

A Confident Petition

This is the confidence we have in approaching God:
that if we ask anything according to his will, he hears us.
And if we know that he hears us—whatever we ask—
we know that we have what we asked of him.

1 JOHN 5:14-15 NIV

In 1 John, we find the bold claim that God will give us what we ask for. We are to take our petitions confidently before God believing he will answer our prayers. So, a new car, a flatter stomach, and a child that behaves immediately and happily just because we want it? Not exactly.

Christians who make this false assumption are bound to end up disappointed and possibly blaming God. This can be especially hard to explain to children. I asked, so why didn't I get? If we simply ask God for what we want when we want it, we are missing the essence of the promise. Take a closer look at the verse. That little phrase, "according to his will," makes all the difference.

When did you last get a no from God? In light of verse 14, why do you think he didn't grant your request? Ask God to fill you with desire for the things he wants you to have. Ask God to bless your children the way he wants to bless them.

Greatness of love

We love because he first loved us.
1 JOHN 4:19 NIV

In the moment we hold our newborn for the first time, a new kind of love washes over us and we get a glimpse of how God loves us. Holding that precious baby is overwhelming and wonderful. We feel at a degree that we have never felt before. It is impossible to define or measure or contain our emotions.

We have the ability to love to such a degree only because God first loved us. He loved us so we could love him and love others. Without him we couldn't know the greatness of love.

Do you know how much you are loved?

Strong Love

Love does not demand its own way.
1 CORINTHIANS 13:5 NLT

It seems there are few passages in the Bible more potent than 1 Corinthians 13. Unfortunately, we hardly listen to the words because we've heard them so many times. It is critical that we are filled with God's love, so we are able to love the children he has given us. His strong love filling our hearts will remove insecurities and self-love so that we can love our children like he does.

God says love does not insist on its own way. He loves us in a way that seeks to serve, and he calls us to love others in the same way. Love is humble, gentle, and protective. When conflict arises in our homes, God calls us to lead our children by loving them. When they are led by love, they will be more apt to respond favorably.

Can you ask God to remove from your heart any calluses related to his simple but profound words? Receive his selfless, strong love today so you can show the same to your children.

Weathering the Storm

*"The rain came down, the streams rose,
and the winds blew and beat against that house;
yet it did not fall, because it had its foundation on the rock."*
MATTHEW 7:25 NIV

As a new or young mother, it is easy to believe that raising your children right will be pretty simple. Play Bible songs in the car, take your children to Sunday School, read to them from their children's Bibles, and they'll grow up knowing, loving, and following Jesus. When your four-year-old boldly and passionately declares their undying love for Jesus, you fist-pump internally. Yes! I've done it! The foundation is laid; the course is set.

Then adolescence hits. That sweet boy may begin to actually dislike going to church. The darling daughter may have some really tough questions and some serious doubts. What now? We wait. We wait, we pray, and we trust.

Where are your children on their individual faith journeys? Share your hopes, fears, and dreams with God. Ask him to build you up so the foundation you lay is strong enough to weather any storm. If you are in the storm right now, throw yourself into his arms. Let him hold you as you wait it out.

Why Wait

They who wait for the LORD shall renew their strength;
they shall mount up with wings like eagles;
they shall run and not be weary;
they shall walk and not faint.
ISAIAH 40:31 ESV

As a general rule, people don't like waiting for anything anymore. This is easily confirmed by observing a line at a coffee shop. People are impatiently scrolling through their phones, sighing repeatedly, frowning, and quietly grumbling if they have to wait two minutes for a latte. We are an instant gratification culture. We put purchases we can't wait to buy, or can't afford, on credit cards.

Gone are the days of snail mail; it's replaced by instant messaging. We don't even take the time to make phone calls anymore, and we grow restless when we don't receive instant replies to our texts. There is growth to be found in trusting in God and his timing.

What blessings do you find during the times you choose to wait on the Lord? God does not ask you to wait for him because he is too busy. He knows there is joy for you in anticipating what is to come.

Perfect Love

There is no fear in love,
but perfect love casts out fear.
For fear has to do with punishment,
and whoever fears has not been perfected in love.
1 JOHN 4:18 ESV

Does your heart get fearful at times? There are many things that can spark fear. If we aren't discerning about the thoughts that go through our minds, fear can consume us. Once fear has settled into our hearts, our actions respond to that fear. It has an awful snowball effect.

When we give our lives to God, he puts a new Spirit within us. This is the same Spirit that raised Christ Jesus from the dead. It isn't a spirit of fear. Satan loves for us to be afraid. He knows that when we are fearful, we are robbed of the peace that comes with our inheritance as God's daughters. God would have us know that his perfect love is strong enough to get rid of all fear.

Are you fearful? There is no fear in love. When your heart becomes afraid, ask God to fill you with his perfect love. Bring your fears to the Father and receive his peace.

The Call for Help

I look up to the hills,
but where does my help come from?
My help comes from the LORD,
who made heaven and earth.
PSALM 121:1-3 NCV

Depending on the type of person you are, you may not be very good at asking for help. There are those who like to be the helpers: they do best serving others because they feel capable and useful. Then there are those who gladly accept service any time they are given the opportunity. Neither is better than the other, and both have their positive elements.

In different seasons of life, natural helpers may need to be the ones receiving help. Sometimes this is hard to accept, and we have to be careful not to let pride take control. Asking for help is part of being vulnerable: we push everything aside to say, "I can't do this alone." God has put capable people in our lives who love to help, but they won't know we need help until we ask.

Can you easily ask for help? God asks you to take a chance on the people he's intricately placed in your life. You'll be amazed at how much stronger you feel when you're leaning on those who want to carry the load with you.

A Lonely Place to Live

Two are better than one,
because they have a good return for their labor:
If either of them falls down,
one can help the other up.
But pity anyone who falls
and has no one to help them up.
ECCLESIASTES 4:9-10 NIV

Sometimes in our own stubbornness and pride we try to do everything on our own. We buy into the lie that we don't need anyone: not the church, not friends, not even God. Usually this attitude is driven by fear or perhaps past hurt and disappointment. We push away everyone who wants to love and help us. It doesn't really work out for us in the end though. God created in us a need for him and a need for others. Even if we are successful in our own pursuits, pride isolates us from God and others. That is a lonely place to live.

If we lay aside our pride and past fears, we are able to commune with others, deeply benefiting from the joy of living together.

What are some things you are trying to do on your own?
Can you see how allowing someone to help
can be a blessing to both of you?

Risk Taker

*Your word is a lamp to guide my feet
and a light for my path.*
PSALM 119:105 NLT

There will be opportunities that arise that might be surprising to us. We might suddenly be presented with something that feels kind of terrifying. We view it as an opportunity because we see the benefit in it somewhere along the way. We understand that it could be as much of a gift to our lives as a potentially difficult ride or transition before the gift appears.

Stepping through the unknown takes courage, and courage isn't always readily available. Through the power of prayer, and wrestling with the opportunity's positives and negatives, hopefully we come to the point where our hearts feel the peace we've been looking for. That makes the task of accepting the opportunity much easier.

Have you taken a risk and been pleasantly surprised by the outcome? How do you fully give your trust to God? You still might not feel brave about a decision, but you can trust the peace in your heart. That alone takes courage. This opportunity might be one of the biggest surprises of your life; it's wonderful and scary, but perfect for you.

Lifestyle of Prayer

Are any of you suffering hardships? You should pray.
Are any of you happy? You should sing praises.
Are any of you sick? You should call for the elders of the church to
come and pray over you, anointing you with oil in the name of the Lord.
Such a prayer offered in faith will heal the sick, and the Lord will make
you well. And if you have committed any sins, you will be forgiven.
JAMES 5:13-15 NLT

Do your children know how and when to pray? James reminds us to take everything—our joys, sorrows, struggles, and triumphs—before God. He wants to lighten our heavy hearts and to heal our broken bodies. He also wants to hear our praises, our joyful songs, when he comes through for us. He wants to forgive us when we don't come through for him.

God is already everywhere around us; he wants to be everything to us.

Do you pray with your children? Do they see or hear you when you pray? Encourage them to take everything to God, and make sure they know you are doing the same. Talk about it together when he answers a prayer.

Chosen for This

*"For I have chosen him, so that he will direct his children
and his household after him to keep the way of the LORD
by doing what is right and just."*
GENESIS 18:19 NIV

Have you ever watched another family and then looked at your own with a completely different lens? Suddenly, the kids you labeled as having personality are now disasters. Nothing can make us diagnose our families worse than comparing them to another family. The behaviors we are now irritated by, we want to correct. The personalities we thought were so cute and refreshing, we want to change. The lies that the enemy wants us to believe start to pile up.

We have to be able to ignore those lies and lean on the truth. If our inner critics are getting the best of us, we can step back into God's grace. Remember, he didn't make a mistake in giving these children to us. He chose us for them. That should help us shift our perspective.

Is there another family that you constantly compare yours to?
Take another look at your family and see that they are perfectly yours.
You are the best mother for them, and you can do a great job if you let
God be your guide.

Not Afraid of Aging

That is why we never give up.
Though our bodies are dying,
our spirits are being renewed every day.
2 CORINTHIANS 4:16 NLT

Aging is part of life. It's funny how the aging process seems to start so slowly and then later in life it gets faster and faster. It would be easy to lose heart if we gauged our aging experience purely by what we saw in the mirror. If we did that, we might begin to fear or hate the aging process.

As we abide with the Lord, aging means we are also maturing. We grow in strength and grace in our knowledge of him. We might not look like we used to, but we also aren't being tossed about. There are many benefits to growing older in Jesus. We are not meant to stay young forever. We are eternal beings that will exist eternally. Because of this, we don't need to despise aging. God is preparing for us an eternal weight of glory beyond all comparison.

Do you dread the aging process? As you age, ask God to give you his perspective. The world won't do you any favors in regard to this issue; therefore, it's really important to have the mind of Christ.

May

"Be strong and brave.
Don't be afraid of them and don't be frightened,
because the Lord your God will go with you.
He will not leave you or forget you."

Deuteronomy 31:6 ncv

Natural Beauty

Ask the animals, and they will teach you,
or the birds in the sky, and they will tell you;
or speak to the earth, and it will teach you,
or let the fish in the sea inform you.
Which of all these does not know
that the hand of the LORD has done this?
In his hand is the life of every creature
and the breath of all mankind.
JOB 12:7-10 NIV

Spending time outside should almost be a daily requirement. There is something about fresh air blowing on your face, hearing the rustling of tree leaves, watching the sun slowly fall bathed in beautiful colors, and the natural chatter of animals that is a constant reminder of the extraordinary world God created. To think how God designed it all is beyond our comprehension, and it's supposed to be!

Much of God is a mystery, but there are pieces of his majestic puzzle that give some understanding to the nature he created. It is seen in the way a colony of ants builds a hill, or ducklings line up to follow their mom, or in the natural rhythm of the changing seasons.

When was the last time you got outside and just observed?
Or rolled down a grassy hill with your kids?
Get outside and play in the beauty he created for you to enjoy!

Love like Jesus

"A new command I give you: Love one another.
As I have loved you, so you must love one another.
By this everyone will know that you are my disciples,
if you love one another."
JOHN 13:34-35 NIV

Jesus showed his love for us by making the ultimate sacrifice. Before that, he made a million other little sacrifices.

Throughout his ministry, Jesus' only need was to do the will of the Father, and the Father's will was that he loved: unselfishly, unreservedly, unwaveringly. His final command to the Apostles? Love. Love like I love you. The first part is easy; the second part may require a bit more work, and a lot more prayer.

Most of the time, it's easy to love your children, but do you love them like Jesus commands? What steps can you take to truly love like Jesus, not just with your kids but in every part of your life?

Acts of Kindness

Love each other like brothers and sisters.
Give each other more honor than you want for yourselves.
ROMANS 12:10 NCV

Small acts of kindness can be deeply impacting. You never know how encouraging a simple act of kindness can be to another mom. Regardless of what is going on around you, try to take the time to reach out to another mom. Invite her in for a cup of coffee and a break from her own chaos. Take her kids off her hands for a morning so she can rest. Write her a letter of encouragement or surprise her with a simple gift *just because*.

We can get so wrapped up in our own hurts and trials that we miss those around us who are in the middle of their own struggles. God wants us to care for the hurting.

No act you do in the name of Jesus Christ is insignificant. Can you see the needs around you? Ask God for insight into your friends' worlds. It doesn't matter how messy you are, you can always reach out to others and help them.

Diverse Voice

A generous person will prosper;
whoever refreshes others will be refreshed.
PROVERBS 11:25 NIV

Sometimes an encouraging phone call, card, or message from a friend comes at exactly the right time. Maybe we've had a tough day with the kids and are feeling worn out when we check our voicemail and hear, "Give yourself time, patience, and grace today." Our eyes fill with tears because someone was thinking about us at the very moment that we didn't want to feel alone. That wasn't by chance.

God uses strangers, neighbors, friends, family, and even our children to convey his message of truth. He bestows wisdom to us in all forms. Usually these messages come as a breath of fresh air at just the time we need them.

Are you that friend for others when they need God to speak through you? Who can you bless today with an encouraging word? When you're on the receiving end, embrace those gifts and take the messages to heart. Let them permeate your soul and breathe life into your lungs, so you can hear his voice amidst the chaos.

Scriptural Advice

Warn those who are lazy. Encourage those who are timid. Take tender care of those who are weak. Be patient with everyone. See that no one pays back evil for evil, but always try to do good to each other and to all people. Always be joyful. Never stop praying. Be thankful in all circumstances, for this is God's will for you who belong to Christ Jesus.

1 Thessalonians 5:14-18 nlt

Paul often writes to the churches he mentored as if they are his children, and much of the advice he gives them is useful for mothers. We spend time trying to teach our children not to be lazy, to speak up for themselves and others, to be patient and kind. We ask them to own their responses and not to react in the same manner if they are mistreated. We tell them to change their grumpy attitudes and to be grateful. It seems we could use a healthy dose of our own advice.

Today, let this passage from 1 Thessalonians encourage and guide your parenting.

Which piece of Paul's counsel most speaks to you as a mother?
Which would be the most difficult to live out?
Share your heart with your Father.

Wildly in Love

I am my beloved's,
And his desire is toward me.
SONG OF SOLOMON 7:10 NKJV

The phrase *Jesus loves you* should cause us to gasp with joy, tremble with relief, and rest with peace. It is the most profound statement in the entire universe. However, when we hear it so often, our ears get dull and we are no longer moved by the greatest truth in all of human history.

Let's remember the love of Jesus today. The creator of the universe is the embodiment of love. His love is strong—*very strong*. It is able to sustain the weight of the entire world's sin. Every horrific, perverse sin was not strong enough to turn God away from mankind forever. He is still consumed with love for his precious creation. Nothing is strong enough to separate us from God's love. It still wins hearts. It still conquers self-doubt and hatred. It silences our accusers. It says, "This is my bride, and I love her!"

Do you know that God is wildly in love with you? Nothing can separate you from his love. Enjoy him today. Let his love conquer your doubt. It is indeed more than able!

Longing for Affirmation

*I am convinced that nothing can ever separate us from God's love.
Neither death nor life, neither angels nor demons, neither our fears for
today nor our worries about tomorrow—not even the powers of hell can
separate us from God's love.*

Children will often test the limits with their parents. They act out, break rules, and push boundaries. This testing is a view inside their hearts. They want to know answers to important questions: "Do you love me?" "How much?" "For always?" They need constant encouragement and affirmation that no matter who they are or what they do, our love and devotion will stay the same. So they test it.

In many ways we are like children. We want affirmation that God will always love us. We push his limits. We test boundaries and may even go as far as walking away from him to see if he will follow. We long to know that his love for us is steadfast and unwavering.

Do you relate to God like a child? Is your heart crying out to be reminded that he loves you now and always will? God is eager to erase your doubts and encourage you that he will always love you. He will go to great lengths to ease your fears.

Real Wisdom

The wisdom from above is first of all pure. It is also peace loving, gentle at all times, and willing to yield to others. It is full of mercy and the fruit of good deeds. It shows no favoritism and is always sincere.

. JAMES 3:17 NLT

The minute an expectant mother begins to show, people—total strangers even—start offering advice and sharing the wisdom they've accumulated through their own years of parenting. Some suggestions, like which stroller to buy or whether cloth or disposable diapers are the way to go, are easily discernible as helpful or not.

When it comes to bigger decisions, matters of the heart and soul, how do we know when to really listen? Here's some great advice from James:

Do you have a more experienced mom you rely on for parenting wisdom? If so, how does her advice fare when held up to these standards? If you do not have someone you rely on, pray God will send you someone with true wisdom.

Shower of Love

Love never gives up,
never loses faith,
is always hopeful,
and endures through every circumstance.
1 CORINTHIANS 13:7 NLT

Everyone makes mistakes. So, friends, be kind to yourselves. Be kind to the daughter you see in the mirror. Be kind to that girl you might not think is worthy of love. Be kind to the mom who is full of imperfections and mistakes. God loves you, inadequacies and all. He sees you through the lens of a Father that loves without conditions or expectations.

We can learn so much from the love of our heavenly Father. It is so important to make every effort to see beyond the situation: beyond mayhem and spilled milk, beyond the colored writing on the wall and the tantrums being thrown on the floor, beyond the outbursts of emotion and breaking of curfews. We can choose to look for the best parts. The gifts entrusted to our care are worth the love and forgiveness we should shower on them every day.

What are the imperfections you see in yourself and your children that you can give up? Show your children more grace by loving them unconditionally. Let them be found saying, "It's okay; I made a mistake, but I'm still loved."

Just a Mom

"Give, and it will be given to you.
A good measure, pressed down,
shaken together and running over,
will be poured into your lap.
For with the measure you use,
it will be measured to you."

LUKE 6:38 NIV

Sometimes we wonder if our efforts as moms are worthwhile. We devote all of our time and energy into loving and teaching the children entrusted into our care. Many times our efforts go unseen, and we feel insignificant in the world's eyes.

The world may see you as "just a mom," but in God's eyes, your job is important. Raising children to be tenderhearted toward God is one of the greatest tasks you can be called to.

Are you aware of how very important your role as a mother is?
Even when your days seem long and endless, when parenting is more
work than blessing, take heart that your job as a mother is valuable.

Faithfulness of Love

I will sing of the LORD's great love forever;
with my mouth I will make your faithfulness
known through all generations.
I will declare that your love stands firm forever,
that you have established your faithfulness in heaven itself.
PSALM 89:1–2 NIV

There is nothing in the universe like God's love. We tend to view God's love through a human filter. When we hear the word *love*, we often have other attributes attached to that word, sometimes even unknowingly. But when God says he loves us, he means love in its purest form. He means unadulterated, undefiled love: love that is never selfish and never has other motives.

His love is remarkably strong. It is able to bear the weight of *everything*. Jesus never cracked or broke on that cross. His love bore the weight of every sin. His love is also entirely steadfast. It never wanes or loses intensity. It is constantly there, never failing amongst the failures of man. He doesn't base his love for us on our love for him. That would be fickle.

Can you take some time to enjoy the faithfulness of God's love?
As you do, you will find it increases your capacity to love others well.

Shepherd's Voice

*"My sheep listen to my voice;
I know them, and they follow me."*
JOHN 10:27 NIV

In the Bible, God's people are sometimes called sheep. The only protection sheep have from predators is to stick together and follow their shepherd. Right from birth, lambs learn quickly to follow the herd. This can be both a positive skillset and a negative one. For our little lambs, it means they are easily influenced by anyone older. This can be a scary thought for a parent in today's world of peer pressure.

Jesus says we should know his voice and follow him. Our job as moms is to help our lambs hear the voice of Jesus. Our job is to teach them to be still so they can hear his whispers. We want them to recognize whose voice they hear. If they hear the voice of Jesus, they will more easily drown out the voices of others and follow him.

What are some practical things you can do to teach your children who Jesus is and how to hear his voice? Your children can learn from a young age to follow the one voice that matters. They will recognize Jesus by the sound of his voice, and he will lovingly lead them on the right path.

Record of Wrongs

Love keeps no record of wrongs.
1 CORINTHIANS 13:5 NIV

Many experts agree that one of the ways to keep relationships healthy and strong is to avoid words like *always* and *never*. True love releases past mistakes and genuinely believes for the best next time. This gives freedom from guilt and permission for the relationship to grow.

This truth applies to everyone we interact with including our sweet children. Let's not keep track of their offenses and label them for their mistakes. Let's give them freedom to grow and learn from their downfalls.

Can you see how this applies to you too? God loves you and keeps no record of your confessed wrongs. Release yourself from regrets and live in God's freedom.

It Is Possible

"Humanly speaking, it is impossible.
But with God everything is possible."
MATTHEW 19:26 NLT

So many of the things God asks of us seem impossible. How are we supposed to raise our children right when we know we ourselves could love more, trust more, give more, and care about ourselves less?

The story of Jesus' encounter with a wealthy young man illustrates this point poignantly. The young man wants to know how to guarantee his place in heaven. Jesus tells him he must give up everything he has. Everything. And this guy has a lot. He leaves devastated; the price is too high to pay. The disciples are concerned, wondering if anyone can actually do enough.

Jesus couldn't say it enough, and you can't hear it enough. You will never please God, and never enter his kingdom, on your own power. Rather than seeing this as a burden, can you allow yourself to see it as a blessing? Admit your weakness over your own sin and thank God for loving you and saving you anyway.

Perfect Peace

*You will keep in perfect peace
all who trust in you,
all whose thoughts are fixed on you!*
ISAIAH 26:3 NLT

Do you find that you are a news junkie always following the latest headline? There are seasons when we might be called to that. Furthermore, it is prudent of us to be aware of the times that we are living in as we await the Lord's return. However, when following the events of the world, it is easy for fear to grip our hearts.

Perfect peace is a tremendous gift from the Lord! God isn't asserting that we can have peace when all is well in the world. His offer of perfect peace applies when everything around us is shaking. We do have a small part to play in this promise though. We are told to keep our minds on him.

Do you have your mind fixed on Christ? When your mind is on him, you become more grounded; you aren't tossed around by the waves of fear and worry. You can enjoy God's promise of stability and peace.

Fostering Love

"You shall teach them diligently to your sons and shall talk of them when you sit in your house and when you walk by the way and when you lie down and when you rise up."
DEUTERONOMY 6:7 NASB

Caring for our children doesn't end at ensuring that they have full bellies and a warm place to sleep at night. Those are just the basics. God asks us to invest in our children in a much deeper, more powerful way by teaching them to love him with all their heart, soul, and mind.

How do we instill this love for God in their hearts? By example. In everything we do and in everything we say, we should demonstrate our devotion to him. During dinner time, driving to school, playing at the park, or shopping at the mall, we should talk about God's goodness. Our homes and lives should center around Jesus.

How are you investing in your child's walk with God? Invite Jesus into your conversations and activities. Foster an atmosphere for your child to seek God in a real and powerful way.

With Him

"If you keep my commandments, you will abide in my love, just as I have kept my Father's commandments and abide in his love. These things I have spoken to you, that my joy may be in you, and that your joy may be full."
JOHN 15:10-11 ESV

Do you know that Jesus wants you with him all the time? He wants you to experience as much joy as you possibly can, so you will bring that joy to others. In John's gospel, Jesus implores his followers: abide in me; stay with me; remain in me. Just as a baby needs its mother to survive, so we need Christ. Without him we can do nothing, but with him our lives bear fruit.

We can find ourselves totally connecting with God one moment, like after a great message at church or as we watch our sleeping children, only to have the connection fade as life's distractions push him aside. We are much more productive and joyful when we spend time in his presence.

What habits can you begin or end in order to abide in him to remain in his presence? Let today be the day your joy begins to be full.

The Fairy Tale

Such things were written in the Scriptures long ago to teach us.
And the Scriptures give us hope and encouragement
as we wait patiently for God's promises to be fulfilled.
ROMANS 15:4 NLT

For moms, days can blend together into weeks. We wake up and repeat the same day seven days a week: cycle after cycle. Sometimes that daily routine becomes mundane, and we can find ourselves in a pity-party pattern. Someone else's life seems better—more exciting, more balanced. This is where we have a choice. We can live a small story that is only about us; it fails to believe in who God is and what he is doing. Our days are mundane, our prayers are empty, and we are fearful, unhappy, and whiny.

Or we can live the story that the Bible promises to us as believers. Christ overcame death. The hard days, the times of suffering, the mundane weeks, are part of our building process to create something good and beautiful. Wisdom is born from uncertainty and confusion. God's voice is tender and loving. Our story is his story, and he determines our every step.

How do you tell the story of God's faithfulness in your life?
That story is a beautiful one to tell your children! It's a story that matters.

Servanthood

*"If I then, your Lord and Teacher, have washed your feet,
you also ought to wash one another's feet."*
JOHN 13:14 NKJV

Most moms take on the brunt of household duties. Scrubbing, mopping, dusting, organizing, and washing clothes… it never ends! Neither do meal planning, grocery shopping, or cooking. It's an exhausting and often thankless job. This is why we need to be extra careful not to let bitterness creep into our hearts.

We serve our families because we love them, but it's easy to forget that day after day with our hands in dirty dishwater. In those times we need to remember Jesus, who humbly knelt before his disciples to wash their feet. What a powerful image.

What is the condition of your heart when you serve your family and household? What can you do to guard yourself against bitterness? Maybe not today, but one day your children will look back and remember your hard work and the example you gave them of Jesus. Every dish you wash, every meal you cook, and each load of laundry has meaning. God is using you to serve your children.

He Sees

*Nothing in all creation is hidden from God.
Everything is naked and exposed before his eyes,
and he is the one to whom we are accountable.*

HEBREWS 4:13 NLT

When you play peek-a-boo with a really small child, they think that if they cover their eyes you can't see them. It's funny, isn't it, that they think they can hide by simply covering their own eyes? When they are a little older, hide and seek is similar. Hiding in plain sight, unable to control their giggles, they believe as long as they don't look at us, we won't see them. Adorable.

Maybe that's how God reacts when we try to hide from him. "Oh, how precious! She thinks because she is pretending to enjoy herself, I can't see how much she's hurting inside." Whatever we are thinking, pretending, ignoring, or forcing ourselves through, God sees our hearts. He knows our pain and he knows our sin, and he wants to take it all away.

Are you hiding in any part of your life? Do you believe that if you haven't confessed something maybe God hasn't noticed it? Spend a few minutes searching yourself for anything you are trying to keep hidden and ask God for the faith to uncover your eyes.

Familiar with Suffering

During Christ's days on earth he pleaded with God, praying with passion and with tearful agony that God would spare him from death. And because of his perfect devotion his prayer was answered and he was delivered. But even though he was a wonderful Son, he learned to listen and obey through all his sufferings.

HEBREWS 5:7-8 TPT

Suffering is a gift from God. Jesus was said to be a *man of suffering*. He was familiar with suffering; it wasn't a foreign concept to him. We can be deeply grateful for that simple fact.

Because Jesus suffered, we can receive tremendous courage when we suffer. Our very own Savior knows what it is like to hurt. Jesus knew who to turn to when all else had left him. He knew who his primary source of encouragement was—his Father. And he knew that suffering would cause him to press in even more to the Father's love and affirmation.

When Jesus tells you to take up your cross and follow him, can you have the assurance that as you do, his leadership will guide you straight into the loving arms of the Father?

God's Voice

"The world cannot accept him,
because it neither sees him nor knows him.
But you know him, for he lives with you and will be in you."
JOHN 14:17 NIV

Many of us wish we could *hear* the voice of God. We might have heard others say, "God told me to…" and we wonder why we can't *hear* his voice like they do. Here is some encouragement for us: we are made in his image. When we confess and follow Jesus as our Lord and Savior, his Spirit comes to live in us. We have to let that seep into our hearts. Even if we've been believers for a long time, we need to listen to that promise again right now; his Spirit is alive *in us*!

We can hear God's voice in different ways. His Spirit speaks to us through our conscience. When we're tempted, that Spirit warns and nudges us to do the right thing. When we're making the right decision, his Spirit pours peace into our hearts.

How do you hear God's voice? You can hear his voice, beloved daughter, you just have practice listening so you can discern how he speaks to you.

Determining Words

A soft answer turns away wrath,
But a harsh word stirs up anger.
PROVERBS 15:1 NKJV

Our words are powerful aren't they? They have the ability to soothe and comfort our little ones. They can encourage and build confidence in our children. They can bring joy and peace to a troubled heart. But they also have the ability to destroy. Words can rip apart families and impart discouragement. They can create wounds and invite anger. They are not easily erased. Words can leave scars.

As moms, we need to be ever careful with what we say and how we say it. It's far too easy to be careless with our words when we are parenting especially when we are tired or frustrated. It is important to take a deep breath and remember that our words have impact. Instead of choosing anger, respond gently and see what happens.

Have you responded to your child in anger recently?
It's not too late to make repairs. Children are quick to forgive.

Managing Time

*Look carefully then how you walk, not as unwise but as wise,
making the best use of the time, because the days are evil.
Therefore do not be foolish, but understand what the will of the Lord is.*
EPHESIANS 5:15-17 ESV

Do you sometimes look at the clock and wonder where the last few hours went? Or stare at your to-do list and wish you could add a few hours to the clock or days to the calendar? Time is short and precious; we know this. Why then is time so difficult to manage and make the most of? In a word: distraction.

We enter a room to put away a wayward stuffed animal then find ourselves coming up for air an hour or more later, having rearranged the closet, the dresser drawers, or even the furniture. We sit down at our computer to respond to a single important email, and hours can disappear in a blink. So, what's the answer? Paul's advice can be broken down into a few steps: look carefully how you walk, make the best use of your time, and understand the will of the Lord.

How can you determine to use Paul's advice
when it comes to managing your time?

A Respectable Job

*"Whoever exalts himself will be humbled,
and whoever humbles himself will be exalted."*
MATTHEW 23:12 ESV

Sweet mother, has the world tarnished the way you view motherhood? In case you hadn't noticed, it's not a position that is highly honored. In fact, it's almost shameful to fully give ourselves to mothering our children. We are expected to do so much more than simply parent. We are expected to also hold down a *respectable job* to show our worth and value.

God wants us to know that he sees us. Every sleepless night, the burn in our muscles from holding our babies, and the monotony of daily chores have not gone unnoticed by him. He sees it all. It is the lifestyle of a servant: always working behind the scenes to make others successful. We must know that servanthood was the very lifestyle he chose for himself.

Do you know that Jesus made himself remarkably low to serve you? Many people don't see what you do, but the one who judges rightly does, and his opinion is all that matters.

Easy Judgment

This is how we know that we belong to the truth and how we set our hearts at rest in his presence: If our hearts condemn us, we know that God is greater than our hearts, and he knows everything. Dear friends, if our hearts do not condemn us, we have confidence before God.

1 JOHN 3:19-21 NIV

Much of our life is spent worrying about how others view us. As moms, we want our kids to obey in public so they are respectful to others, but also so we look like we're in control. We live in a society where judgment comes easily. Unfortunately, that means we judge ourselves just as effortlessly. When our children misbehave, the enemy creeps in to show us just how bad things have become.

Our encouragement today is that the enemy lies. We have to protect our hearts. Pruning our hearts before the Lord requires patience, love, and some work. We can't let others or ourselves be the judge of who God created us to be.

Have you become your own worst critic? Instead of judging your every thought and action, spend time in his presence and hear his sacred message for you: you are loved, adored, and precious in his sight.

In His Strength

I can do all things through him
who strengthens me.
PHILIPPIANS 4:13 ESV

Do you ever feel unqualified for something God has called you to?
Maybe your job is overwhelming. Perhaps you feel like an opportunity
given is way over your head. Maybe motherhood feels like a major
undertaking, and you aren't certain you qualify for such a high calling.

It doesn't matter what we face, we can conquer it with God's strength.
With his help there's nothing we cannot accomplish and accomplish well.
He will guide us and give us the tools to finish strong. We can lean on
him in these times for strength.

How are you living your life? Do you trust that in every situation God is
holding you? Are you depending on yourself to follow through or are you
depending on God?

All by Myself

"Teach them to faithfully follow all that I have commanded you.
And never forget that I am with you every day,
even to the completion of this age."
MATTHEW 28:20 TPT

"Mommy, I can do it all by myself!" From an early age, our children start to show us their independence and stubbornness. This only gets worse as they get older. They are growing up, perhaps even more stubborn or independent than they were at age three, and we have no choice but to give up control.

In the same way our children pull away, we often try to pull away from our Father: "I got this. I can definitely do it on my own." So, we go about our day, trying to do it all ourselves, recognizing at some point that it isn't manageable. We can't do it on our own because he is still holding us. But he continues to shower us with grace even when we resist. What a faithful, loving, patient Father we serve!

Does the phrase, "I can do it myself," look different to you now? Don't resist God's help. It's not worth it. Admit that you need him and enjoy the benefit of relying on him to meet your needs.

Lifegiving Friendships

*An enemy might defeat one person,
but two people together can defend themselves;
a rope that is woven of three strings is hard to break.*

ECCLESIASTES 4:12 NCV

God designed us for friendship. Consider Jesus; he shared the whole of his life with his closest friends. A group of women to pray with, share highs and lows with, and seek Godly counsel from is an essential part of the Christian life, but the busier our family lives become, the more challenging it can be to maintain close friendships.

Playdates, carpools, practices, and errands take over our schedules and suddenly we realize we haven't seen our girlfriends in weeks—or months. If this is you, it's time for a coffee date or girl's night.

What lifegiving friendships do you need to nurture? If you find yourself in a lonely season, ask God to send you some friends, and then keep your eyes open.

Generosity of Time

*Each of you should give what you have decided in your heart to give,
not reluctantly or under compulsion, for God loves a cheerful giver.*
2 CORINTHIANS 9:7 NIV

Sometimes it is easier to be generous with our money than our time. Life is usually so busy that we tend to guard our time religiously. Often we get so focused on ourselves and our own to-do list that we fail to notice the needs around us. Perhaps a friend could use a phone call, or an elderly neighbor help with planting her garden. Maybe volunteer hours could be a blessing to your child's teacher, or someone at church who needs help moving.

We are called to be the hands and feet of Christ. There are so many opportunities to serve others around us, and there are such blessings to be found when we do.

Sometimes giving of yourself is more valuable than a hastily written check. God loves a cheerful giver. Can you be that cheerful giver, even if it means laying aside your own schedule? Think about how you could bless someone with your time.

A Sad Day

Why, my soul, are you downcast?
Why so disturbed within me?
Put your hope in God,
for I will yet praise him,
my Savior and my God.

PSALM 42:11 NIV

Even the most blessed of mothers with the most angelic babies, the most obedient and over-achieving children, and the most doting and helpful friends will occasionally have a day of inexplicable sadness.

When those days come, and if counting our blessings doesn't take away the ache, we can consider this: as beautiful as our lives are, there is still something better to come. This is not our home. Perhaps we are missing our Father.

What is your typical response to the unexplained ache that sometimes comes upon your otherwise happy heart? Do you find yourself feeling ungrateful or even guilty on a sad day? Turn to God, allow yourself to feel low, and thank him for the reminder that he is the only one who can truly satisfy you.

June

Take delight in the LORD,

and he will give you your heart's desires.

Commit everything you do to the LORD.

Trust him, and he will help you.

PSALM 37:4-5 NLT

Cinderella and Prince Charming

When you make a vow to God, do not delay to fulfill it.
He has no pleasure in fools; fulfill your vow.
It is better not to make a vow
than to make one and not fulfill it.

ECCLESIASTES 5:4-5 NIV

Whether we have sons or daughters, there is an expectation that when they fall in love, it will be a forever kind of love. Disney rnovies and fairy tale romances have our kids believing their spouses will fall out of the sky looking incredibly dashing. They won't have baggage, they won't have sin, and they won't have bad days where they question their purpose. These perfect people will be kind to everyone and generous to all.

Our children may be buying into the lie that marriage should be perfect. In doing so, they are setting themselves up for a difficult road. But there is hope. We can teach them God's blueprint for marriage. Marriage was the idea of our Father. He designed marriage and knows exactly what it needs to thrive.

Are you comfortable speaking with your children about the expectations of marriage? Encourage your children that they need to be committed to their future spouse through the beauty and the trial that marriage can bring. Help them set their expectations with God's parameters.

Joy in Circumstance

The LORD was with him; he showed him kindness and granted him favor in the eyes of the prison warden. The warden paid no attention to anything under Joseph's care, because the LORD was with Joseph and gave him success in whatever he did.

GENESIS 39:21, 23 NIV

Dropped into a well, sold into slavery by his own brothers, jailed in the wake of false accusations, Joseph has a thing or two to teach us about faith and perseverance. The next time the frustrations, pressures, and even heartbreaks of motherhood overwhelm you, perhaps Joseph's story can inspire you to hang in there, and maybe even find a little joy. Joseph loved God with his whole heart, so he felt his presence all the time. This presence allowed him to experience joy in the unlikeliest of places and in the worst of circumstances.

Circumstances don't matter as much when God is with us. We've seen the joy in the eyes of a Christian Haitian or African. That joy certainly isn't coming from the poverty, disease, and devastation all around them. It's coming from their hearts, and it is available to us as well. If God could help Joseph thrive in prison, surely he can help us in our present situations.

Can you lift up your concerns to God today?
Be bold and ask him for the joy that transcends all circumstances.

Afraid of Monsters

*I sought the LORD, and he answered me
and delivered me from all my fears.
Those who look to him are radiant,
and their faces shall never be ashamed.*

PSALM 34:4-5 ESV

As children we were fearful of monsters under the bed, or we were frightened by the thought of what could be lurking in the dark corners of the room. As irrational as those fears were, they were real to us. We froze, dared not to breathe or cry out, shut our eyes tightly bidding sleep to come. The nights and the darkness they brought seemed endless.

As adults we still fear monsters; however, these days they take the form of an irate boss, difficulty with a relationship, an unfavorable medical diagnosis, or a credit card bill. Fear grips us in a real and powerful way, immobilizing us. If we aren't careful, fear can destroy our peace of mind.

What are the monsters that you fear? As a child of God, you can cry out to him, confident that he will help. You can shake fear and know that whatever monster you face, you don't face it alone.

Quiet Waters

The LORD is my shepherd,
I shall not want.
He makes me lie down in green pastures;
He leads me beside quiet waters.
He restores my soul.
PSALM 23:1-3 NASB

If your kids are young, your house likely isn't quiet. Their many noises, while precious, can make for a frenzied atmosphere. There might be times that their laughter is music to your ears, for it means they aren't sick or sullen. But there are other times that you might feel like you are going crazy from all the noise.

On those days, we have to let him lead us to quiet waters. We know that he is our shepherd. He says we are like sheep. Without a shepherd, sheep wander. We, by nature, won't get the rest we need, so he makes it his job to take us to places of rest. He knows how to lead us to the still, quiet waters.

Literally speaking, your quiet waters might still be quite loud.
But God knows if he can quiet your mind and your thoughts,
you will receive the lifegiving rejuvenation that only he can provide.

In the Secret

"When you pray, do not be like the hypocrites, for they love to pray standing in the synagogues and on the street corners to be seen by others. Truly I tell you, they have received their reward in full. But when you pray, go into your room, close the door and pray to your Father, who is unseen. Then your Father, who sees what is done in secret, will reward you."

MATTHEW 6:5-6 NIV

Cherish the secret things. So much of our life is lived for others. Whether it is the requirement of jobs, raising children, or the programs we volunteer for, so much of our time and energy is spent on other people.

God wants our time. He wants it for us and for him. Maybe this will require a designated prayer closet, or a distant quiet place. Maybe we head outside with our Bible and journal to sneak away for a while. However we do it, our heavenly Father sees us. What a faithful gift that thought alone is; he sees us in secret and will meet us where we are.

Can you get away today in secret to pray? In secret, God will reward your heart. Make sneaking away with him a daily routine.

Transparency

Perfume and incense bring joy to the heart,
and the pleasantness of a friend
springs from their heartfelt advice.
PROVERBS 27:9 NIV

It is okay to cry over spilled milk. It really is. We all have hard days: days where we wake up late, we lose the keys, we can't find matching socks, and then the milk spills! We have those days where we just want to throw in the towel and call it quits. As moms, we think we have to have it all together all the time. We don't though. It is okay to be transparent with each other. By doing so we allow others to love us, encourage us, and pray for us.

Sharing our struggles not only lessens our burdens but reinforces the fact that we are not alone. It also gives permission for our fellow moms to be transparent as well.

Do you feel like you need to be perfect? You don't. Be transparent with a friend today and reap the benefits of sharing your struggles.

They'll Come Around

With meekness you'll be able to carefully enlighten those who argue with you so they can see God's gracious gift of repentance and be brought to the truth.

2 TIMOTHY 2:25 TPT

Proverbs 22:6 might be the single most popular verse in the Bible regarding parenting: "Train children to live the right way, and when they are old, they will not stray from it." It's extremely comforting when our kids are little, happily attending Sunday school, singing Bible songs in their car seats; it's easy then to believe they'll grow up dedicated to their faith and to the values you are teaching them.

Then they get a little older. More often than anyone wants to admit, many children go through a spiritual rebellion; a number of them walk away from their faith entirely. Now what?

No matter their age, what can you do today to point your children in the right direction? How can you gently instruct them in the truth, so it's a path they will know and love and return to?

Knowing Him More

The LORD directs the steps of the godly.
He delights in every detail of their lives.
Though they stumble, they will never fall,
for the LORD holds them by the hand.
PSALM 37:23–24 NLT

Don't you picture the most serene, quiet setting when you hear about a *secret place*? Maybe it's in a field where you sit by yourself, waiting for the Lord to encounter you. Or maybe it's on a porch where everything else has vanished.

Hopefully, whatever we picture, we see us and Jesus together, having a conversation. That is his desire. When we take time to be still, to sit in silence, he will meet us. We will hear his promises for our lives and get to know him at a deeper level. The hustle and bustle of daily life needs to vanish, and we need to meet him in quiet to hear his whisper.

Can you sit in silence today? Take some time to be in his presence. It isn't something that comes naturally, so give yourself patience and practice. Sitting in silence takes skill, and skill needs to be sharpened.

Love Never Fails

God, being rich in mercy, because of the great love with which he loved us, even when we were dead in our trespasses, made us alive together with Christ—by grace you have been saved— and raised us up with him and seated us with him in the heavenly places in Christ Jesus, so that in the coming ages he might show the immeasurable riches of his grace in kindness toward us in Christ Jesus.

EPHESIANS 2:4-7 ESV

Often unintentionally, we place human qualities on God's attributes—we make him in *our* image. Many of us find it almost impossible to believe that God's love is pure. We can't imagine completely selfless love. That is because we assume he is like us. But he isn't.

God's love *never fails*. It will never cease. It is impenetrable; it has no weak points where it will eventually break.

Do you see how you can diminish God's love by assuming he loves like a human? His love was what caused him to create the earth and save the world. It is the totality of all that he is, and it will never fail you no matter what you have done.

Desire to Be Known

O Lord, You have searched me and known me.
You know when I sit down and when I rise up;
You understand my thought from afar.

PSALM 139:1-2 NASB

Do you desire to be known? Most of us do. It is in us to crave deep connections with people and with God. We long for others to know us completely: what we like and don't like, what is in our hearts, and what we fear. We want to share our stories and be understood. It is frustrating and lonely when we're not.

God knows us completely. He understands us in ways no one else can. How wonderful it is to be known and loved by Jesus Christ.

Are you aware of how much God adores you? He not only calls you by name but knows the inner workings of your heart and soul. You are known, and you are deeply loved.

A Daughter

"I am the LORD, your God, the Holy One of Israel, your Savior.
I gave Egypt as a ransom for your freedom;
I gave Ethiopia and Seba in your place.
Others were given in exchange for you.
I traded their lives for yours because you are precious to me.
You are honored, and I love you."
ISAIAH 43:3-4 NLT

We are mothers, but we are also daughters. Every day, no matter what you face, remember whose you are. He called you by name; he chose you. Remember how much he loves you.

Read these verses from Isaiah out loud; make them yours, and then share your doubts and your gratitude with your Father.

Cheerleaders

*May the God who gives endurance and encouragement give you
the same attitude of mind toward each other that Christ Jesus had.*
ROMANS 15:5 NIV

"Come on, buddy, you can do it. Just a little bit further!" Ah, the sweet
sound of an older sibling nurturing a younger one: showing them the
ropes, encouraging them in their endeavors, leading them. It's best when
these moments are heard from afar. Our older children are getting it!
They understand that they're leaders, that being kind is so much more
fun than not, that encouragement is invaluable.

In this same way, let us encourage one another in our faith. Imagine our
Abba Father's joy when he sees us lifting one another up in praise and
love. There is so much to be gained in relationship with other believers,
whether on the receiving or giving end.

What are some ways you can encourage others? Think of the delight in
God's heart when he sees you giving your time and talents.

Face of Kindness

"Come," my heart says, "seek his face!"
Your face, LORD, do I seek.
Do not hide your face from me.
PSALM 27:8-9 NRSV

Do you ever long to see God's face? Do you wonder what it looks like when he looks at you? Be assured, his eyes are more gentle than you expect. His expression is more tender than you thought, and his posture is more approachable than you perceived. This isn't just a cute idea. We know it is true because we know what he looked like when he walked the earth. We have direct accounts of how he responded to people with humble hearts. He welcomed them and gave them words that brought freedom.

Picture the nicest person you know: the person who never seems to be bothered by anything and listens attentively to everyone. While that person might be noteworthy in their godliness, they are only a mere reflection of the kindness of God. He is even better.

Do you know that God never has a bad day?
He is consistent in his love for you. Ask him for a picture of his face.
It is more approachable than you think.

Human Contact

Now that you have purified yourselves by obeying the truth so that you have sincere love for each other, love one another deeply, from the heart.
1 PETER 1:22 NIV

Many chain restaurants now have little electronic tablets on the tables. These can be used for browsing the menu, buying games for kids to play, or paying the bill at the end of dinner. We should ponder this for a moment. We've gone out to eat with our families to enjoy some time together, and there's that tablet, threatening to steal all that precious time away with a touch of the screen.

When we can't spend a few moments interacting with each other before our food is served, it does seem like we're missing out on an important piece of human existence. In a world of plentiful electronic devices, holding on to some sacred pieces of togetherness might be necessary.

How do you ensure that your family spends time together? You don't need to deny yourself every convenience of modern technology, but can you find an area or two that you can keep to yourselves as a family? Real time together is necessary for good relationships.

Carried

He takes care of his people like a shepherd.
He gathers them like lambs in his arms
and carries them close to him.
He gently leads the mothers of the lambs.
ISAIAH 40:11 NCV

Whether awake or asleep, our hearts and thoughts are often centered on our children. Motherhood is heavy. We worry about making the best decisions. We hope that our love and care is enough. We strive to teach our children the ways they should go. We fight to protect their hearts and minds. Children captivate our time and our energy.

Parenting is wonderful, amazing, and exhausting. But there is rest. God carries us through the storms of motherhood. When our arms are heavy with children, he holds us. When we need answers and direction, he guides us. In his gentleness he loves and cares for us. He knows the battle is tough, and he will carry us through it. As we tend to our children, he is tending to us.

Do you know that God carries you? You aren't alone in mothering, and your burdens are his. Let him release you from those burdens now.

Mercies Anew

Because of the LORD's great love we are not consumed,
for his compassions never fail.
They are new every morning;
great is your faithfulness.

<small>LAMENTATIONS 3:22-23 NIV</small>

A morning will come, if it hasn't already, where you will throw your hands up and say, "I blew it this morning. My child was rude and ungrateful, and I was rude right back. I forgot selflessness, humility, and unconditional love." Or you could put it in fewer words and say, "I was human today."

Only God is perfect. Only Jesus never sinned. Only the Spirit can give us the strength to die to ourselves and live for him. As a mother, living for him looks a lot like living for *them*, and sometimes they don't appreciate us. At all. That can be tough to take, causing feelings of hurt and provoking words of anger. Thankfully, we serve a God who forgives us the moment the thoughts enter our heads, and the second the words leave our mouths.

Have you blown it recently? It's in your past. It's not who you are. This is how great our God is: not just every day brings new mercies; every hour, every minute is an opportunity to start again. We fail and fail again, but his compassion never does.

The Servant Heart

You have been called to live in freedom, my brothers and sisters.
But don't use your freedom to satisfy your sinful nature.
Instead, use your freedom to serve one another in love.
GALATIANS 5:13 NLT

Some days it feels like a whistle might work well in a household: a whistle to stop the kids from fighting, a whistle to get someone's attention, a whistle so the noise stops. *A whistle so we feel heard.* Having a servant heart isn't easy, but, as a mother, it's required. Be assured there is joy to be found in a servant's heart.

The Bible says that through love we are called to serve. It also says with our freedom in Christ we aren't meant to satisfy the desires of our flesh. We serve one another selflessly, without complaining or grumbling. We serve because we love. It's a beautiful thought. Every time we get on the floor and wrestle with our kids, or play a game, or serve a meal, we are showing them tangible, undeniable love.

Did you know that when you serve, you are showing love? Remind yourself of that in the mundane details of today and allow the Lord to fill you with his joy as you continue to serve those placed in your care.

Everything to Everyone

God is able to provide you with every blessing in abundance,
so that by always having enough of everything,
you may share abundantly in every good work.
2 Corinthians 9:8 nrsv

The demands of motherhood are relentless. Someone always needs us, yet we are still human. We need rest, we need sleep, and we need time and strength to care for others and for ourselves. Sometimes it can feel like other people's needs are pressing so tightly into us that we can't breathe.

It is impossible to do it all for, or be it all to, everyone. Eventually something has to give. When that happens, we feel discouraged. It is easy to become overwhelmed with expectations—ours and others'. We need to give ourselves permission to not be everything to everyone. Because we can't. God can. We shouldn't try to take on his role. He doesn't need us to.

Do you feel overwhelmed? Let it go and be encouraged that God knows what you need. When you feel like you can't manage, you should remember that God can. And he will help you.

Not a Result of Works

By grace you have been saved through faith.
And this is not your own doing; it is the gift of God.
EPHESIANS 2:8 ESV

When it's still and quiet, take a moment to remember your salvation. Enjoy the finished work of the cross. Often when we first get saved, we seem to understand that it is purely God's power that has saved us and no effort of our own. As time goes on, we begin to walk away from old sinful behaviors, but something subtle and entirely wicked often takes place in our hearts.

We begin to believe that we have some merit on our own (apart from Christ's work) that makes us desirable to the Father. We believe, at least in part, that we save ourselves by our good records of sinlessness. This makes us self-righteous and proud. The opposite can be true as well: if we struggle with a besetting sin, we believe we aren't received by God.

God saved you fully and completely by his power alone not by your own merit. You don't need to continue trying to earn it. Because of that, you can rest from your works and your self-hatred. Simply pause to enjoy him.

Brave Dependence

*"I have told you all this so that you may have peace in me.
Here on earth you will have many trials and sorrows.
But take heart, because I have overcome the world."*

JOHN 16:33 NLT

When you become a parent for the first time, you understand fear in a whole new way. No longer are you concerned just for yourself, you suddenly have this little person that you are *responsible* for. It is no wonder the concept of helicopter parenting has developed. Parents hover, too fearful to let their kids fail, wanting to protect them from everything that could possibly harm them.

As we become more like Jesus, we go a not-so-pretty process of possible failure, struggle, danger, loss, and disappointment. The promising part of transformation is that God wants to help us, and our children, through it! We have to be willing to lead our children with Godly wisdom and help them navigate the real world with grace. We can't shield them from everything, so we need to gradually let go.

Can you be brave enough to let go a little? Start small. Trust your Father with your children and learn to let them fall while depending on him. Let them live a life with real people, situations, and emotions, discovering that God shows up like he promises.

Proud or Pride

*As for me, may I never boast about anything
except the cross of our Lord Jesus Christ.
Because of that cross, my interest in this world has been crucified,
and the world's interest in me has also died.*

GALATIANS 6:14 NLT

There has never been a more charming, talented, intelligent child than yours. Just ask you. It's true; your child is wonderful. Our children are wonderful. Whether it's a soccer trophy, or cutting a tooth without crying, we're proud of them, and justifiably so. These amazing little beings came from us. It's a miracle that never stops being miraculous.

When does being proud of our children become the sin of pride? We have to check our hearts. Are we comparing our children to others, or boasting to gain status and put others in their place? According to Paul, who had plenty of accomplishments to tout, there's only one thing worth boasting about, and that's our salvation.

What are some of the most special things about your children? Ask God to help you appreciate the incredible people they are without getting wrapped up in worldly competition. Tell Jesus how much his sacrifice means to you.

A Mustard Seed

*"If you have faith like a grain of mustard seed,
you will say to this mountain, 'Move from here to there,'
and it will move, and nothing will be impossible for you."*
MATTHEW 17:20 ESV

Just because something is difficult, it doesn't mean that it's not what God has planned for us. When we hit roadblocks, it's not always a sign that we are heading down the wrong path. It is so easy to start thinking like this when things don't go our way. We must have faith.

Nothing is impossible with God. If our journeys aren't exactly what we imagined, or we're feeling doubt, we need to give it to God. Trust that a little faith, will allow us to move mountains: we can have faith that there is joy in the journey and a plan for our lives. Sometimes, the uphill battle might be the only way to get to the end. But we will come out stronger, more faith-filled, more passionate, and more trusting on the other side.

Do you believe that faith as small as a mustard seed can truly move mountains? Meditate on that for a few minutes.

Power of Words

*The words of a good person give life, like a fountain of water,
but the words of the wicked contain nothing but violence.*
PROVERBS 10:11 NCV

What's the most hurtful thing anyone ever said to you? Most of us can recall at least a short list pretty quickly, and often something said by our parents rests near the top. Even if you came from a loving home, chances are you were dealt some harsh words, and they stuck with you. Now quickly, what are some of the most affirming, encouraging words you've ever heard? Again, most of us can call to mind a well-timed compliment or encouragement, even from many years ago.

As parents, the words we say carry opportunity and responsibility. We can bring life and positivity, or we can bring the sting of insult.

Do you remember some of the hurtful things you've said to your children? Do they remember? How often do you speak words of love, life, and encouragement over them? Do they know how amazing they are? Tell them.

Perfect Presence

You will seek me and find me,
when you seek me with all your heart.
JEREMIAH 29:13 ESV

Remember when your babies started to show you their true smile? You were certain it wasn't gas this time because it looked more genuine. Throughout the day, anytime you saw someone new, you immediately used your magic mom voice to show off the precious smile. The next morning, you could barely wait to start all over again because smiles like that made your heart swell.

Initially, it's our voices that cause those smiles. It's a wonderful, soothing voice of protection and love that our children recognize immediately in a crowd. It's a voice that quickly becomes an important source of connection. This is a great picture of how we connect with our heavenly Father. When we hear his voice, we feel peace, we feel loved, we feel cared for. When we don't understand his voice, or think he is pulling away from us, our joy can quickly turn to fear and uncertainty. But God is never absent.

Don't mistake God's patience for his absence. His timing is perfect and his presence is constant. Smile today, knowing you have the very best Father walking alongside you.

Bravery

"Remember that I commanded you to be strong and brave. Don't be afraid, because the Lord your God will be with you everywhere you go."

JOSHUA 1:9 NCV

What does it mean to be brave? It means we step out of our comfort zones and trust God to protect and guide us. We live a life without fear. We confront the sin in our life head on, believing that God will overcome everything that threatens to destroy us. We seek to repair and restore broken relationships. We leave the past behind and face the future with a smile. We allow ourselves to be defined only by God. We stand uprightly and allow his truth to wash away our sin.

It sounds wonderful and terrifying! We cannot be truly brave on our own. We need God to be our strength. How incredibly privileged we are that God actually *wants* to be our strength.

Where does your strength come from? Your strength comes from the Lord of all creation. He put the stars in the sky and breathed life into mankind. Allow that truth to make you brave today.

To What End

*His mother said to him, "My son, let the curse fall on me.
Just do what I say; go and get them for me."*
GENESIS 27:13 NIV

How far would you go for your children? In Genesis, we are introduced to Rebekah, a mother willing to sacrifice her entire future for her favorite son. Isaac and Rebekah had twin sons. Esau came out first so, by law, was to receive the generational blessing along with the majority of his father's considerable wealth. This suited their father just fine, as Esau's manly ways and adventurous spirit made him Isaac's favorite. But Rebekah preferred Jacob, who had been born just seconds later, clinging to the heel of his twin.

God had told Rebekah that Jacob would be the greater of her two sons, so she had to find a way around tradition. She devised a plan to trick Isaac, but Jacob was hesitant to go along with it. Rebekah, determined to get what she wanted and anxious to ensure God's plan was fulfilled, would not be swayed.

What do you take away from the story of Rebekah and Jacob: an example of a mother's selfless love or a story of conniving and lying to achieve selfish ends? Can both lessons be taught through the story of this family? What would you give up for your own children? What is going too far?

A Wise Investment

They should be rich in good works and generous to those in need, always being ready to share with others. By doing this they will be storing up their treasure as a good foundation for the future so that they may experience true life.
1 TIMOTHY 6:18-19 NLT

Moms of young children often seem to be physically exhausted. Their labor is physical because there are very few things young children can do on their own. When mothers make their children's needs a priority, they are likely putting some of their ambitions and goals on hold. Some days this might not bother them at all. But perhaps there are days when they are filled with a sinking question: "Am I giving my time to the right thing?"

Dear mothers, we have chosen a worthy role. Raising children is a task that is to be esteemed highly. We are giving up on other things, but we should also consider all that we are gaining and investing in. The older we get, the more we seem to value this opportunity. It's like we can see that it was the wisest investment we could have made.

Be encouraged, God values your role as a mother.
Let him guide you and inspire you as you invest in your children.

Upside-down Lens

Set your minds on things above, not on earthly things.
For you died, and your life is now hidden with Christ in God.

COLOSSIANS 3:2-3 NIV

It is possible to change our perspective. An early discovery with mirrored lenses proved that it was possible to get used to a world where everything was upside down. It just took a little time to adjust.

Our brains—the brains God designed specifically for us—are able to change our way of thinking quite quickly. With just a few shifts in perspective, our brains can be rewired. This should give us hope whether we struggle with worry or anxiety, or we focus more on the negative than the positive. We *can* change our perspective with determination and practice.

What can you do, practically speaking, to shift your perspective in a positive way? With prayer, and an upside-down lens, you can start to clearly see your blessings and focus less on what you don't have.

Setting the Tone

A cheerful heart is a good medicine,
but a downcast spirit dries up the bones.
PROVERBS 17:22 NRSV

"If Mama isn't happy, no one is happy." It's an old statement packed with truth. We mothers tend to set the tone in our household. We're in such a unique position to demonstrate God's love. What a huge responsibility. We are much more than caretakers; we are joy givers. We have the ability through our words and actions to emanate his love to our children, in a way that no one else can.

Every smile, every hug, every prayer given is completely impacting. Our attitudes are being studied; our mannerisms are learned and copied. Do we radiate his love through our parenting? Are our homes joyful places to be? Joy is contagious, but so is a sour attitude.

Take a moment to evaluate the tone you are setting in your home. Does it communicate God's love and joy? Sometimes it's hard to be joyful. Some days it is difficult to choose thankfulness. But it's important that we try our best and depend on God for strength when we are weak.

Discipline for Joy

Discipline your children, and they will give you peace of mind
and will make your heart glad.
When people do not accept divine guidance, they run wild.
But whoever obeys the law is joyful.
Words alone will not discipline a servant;
the words may be understood, but they are not heeded.
PROVERBS 29:17-19 NLT

Drop in on a mom's group or even just two mothers talking together, and you are bound to hear talk of discipline. How much correction is needed, how much is too much, and what is the best way to deliver it?

It's no fun to punish a child of any age, but showing our children that actions have consequences is one of the most loving things we can do for them. The Bible has much to say on the subject; the proverbs are particularly rich with encouragement. According to these verses, the outcome of parental discipline is peace for you and joy for them. Who doesn't want more of that?

Do you think of discipline as love? When you must deliver consequences, have you considered that you are setting your children up for a more joyful life?

July

If anyone belongs to Christ,
there is a new creation.
The old things have gone;
everything is made new!

2 Corinthians 5:17 NCV

Glorious Splendor

On the glorious splendor of your majesty,
and on your wondrous works, I will meditate.
PSALM 145:5 NRSV

When you have those days and your kids seem extra squirmy, it's nice to be able to send them outside, isn't it? With a little run through the grass and some sunshine, they can usually turn their attitude around and burn off some steam. They come in with sun-kissed cheeks and sweat in their hair, but they have that glow that says they have breathed in life, smiled at the sun, and felt the breeze on their face.

We moms can so easily go through the motions that we forget to slow down. We forget about this incredibly beautiful world that our Creator made for us to explore. It is amazing what a walk with a friend, or a run through the woods, can do to our soul. God created us as beings who need air, sunshine, and the observation of his incredibly beautiful nature.

Do you take time to get outside and enjoy all that he created? The next time you're feeling a bit squirmy, slow down, take a walk outside, and soak in his presence that's all around you: in the grass between your toes, in the rustle of leaves above you, and in the sunshine kissing your cheeks.

Enough

A capable wife who can find?
She is far more precious than jewels.
PROVERBS 31:10 NRSV

Have you ever walked into a room full of women and felt like you were being sized up? The message isn't always subtle: *you are not enough.* Sadly, the world is quick to display our faults and deem us unworthy or incapable. Our efforts appear futile. There are so many that are eager to criticize.

We can't listen to those voices. Trying to measure up to the world's standards is not only exhausting, it's impossible. Listening to the lies will destroy us. Instead we should set our confidence in Jesus Christ, the one who says, "You *are* enough." He called each of us to motherhood, and he says that we are wonderful.

Are you listening to the world's definition of you? You are a beautiful child of God who, by his grace, is perfectly capable to carry out the task he has created you for. Carry on, beloved, and believe that through him you are more than enough, you are priceless, you are worthy, you are strong.

Afraid of the Dark

The Lord is my light and my salvation—
whom shall I fear?
The Lord is the stronghold of my life—
of whom shall I be afraid?
PSALM 27:1 NIV

"Mommy, will you leave the light on?" Many young children (and more than a few not-so-young ones) fear the dark. Why do you suppose that is? Though nothing bad may have ever happened to them in the dark, they instinctively recoil from places where they can't see.

Perhaps we are not crazy about the dark, either. Whether it is a pile of Legos in our path or an imagined scary monster, we like to know what to expect, and we want the opportunity to avoid danger. God *is* that opportunity. Jesus is the light of the world, and he is a light that never burns out or grows dim. We have nothing to fear.

Find a dark place, the darkest you can find. Sit quietly in the darkness and see what fears or insecurities come to mind, then recite this verse. Imagine the Lord as a light, illuminating every corner of the space you occupy. Seeing clearly, give your fears to him, one by one.

Freedom

The Lord is the Spirit,
and wherever the Spirit of the Lord is,
there is freedom.
2 CORINTHIANS 3:17 NLT

Do we realize the depth of the freedom we have received because of Christ? Jesus came to set the captives free. Free from what? Free from the sin that so easily entangles us. Free from the shame that weighs us down. Free from guilt over our already confessed sins. We were set free to love him and live for him.

Do we live like we are free, or are there things that we are slaves to? It is easy to have imposed on us, or to impose on others, requirements that we think God makes. We have a propensity to love rules and regulations, but many, if not most, of those rules and regulations God does not require us to keep.

Do you know that Christ set you free to enjoy his completed work on the cross? You need not earn it or strive to maintain his work. He said, "It is finished." May the God of all comfort fill your heart with a renewed ability to enjoy your freedom.

Be Perfect

"If you love only those who love you,
what reward is there for that?
Even corrupt tax collectors do that much.
If you are kind only to your friends,
how are you different from anyone else?
Even pagans do that.
Be perfect, therefore,
as your heavenly Father is perfect."
MATTHEW 5:46-48 NLT

Mixed in with all the encouragement, all the unconditional love and acceptance from the Sermon on the Mount, is this impossible command: *Be perfect.* Why would Jesus say this, knowing we are powerless to comply? Don't we spend endless energy helping our children understand they are loved and wonderful just as they are? Don't we try to internalize that message for ourselves?

Taken out of context, this verse can be overwhelming, discouraging, and even alienating. However, when we visit the entire passage we see what Jesus is really asking of us. God loves everyone he ever created. The best way to show your love for him is to do the same.

Who do you struggle to love? How about your children? It starts early with battles over toys, and it only gets more challenging. Share your thoughts with God on loving the unlovable and ask him to guide you through this vital lesson with your children.

Time with God

Give all your worries to him,
because he cares about you.
1 PETER 5:7 NCV

A mother's time is not her own. It belongs to her family and her home. This is especially true when children are young and completely dependent on mom for everything. Time with God is a real need. Carving out that time in our day is a struggle. At the end of the day, all we crave is our soft bed and sleep. The truth is we can't wait for quiet to happen.

God is always there. How wonderful that we don't need to be physically alone to be alone with God. Talk to him while you are bathing your babies, washing dishes, driving carpools, and mopping the floor. He loves to listen. Our devotional times may look different now that we are mothers, but the need for God remains the same.

Do you find it a struggle to connect with God as a mom? Time with him will restore and refresh you. It's more essential than that third or fourth cup of coffee in the middle of the day.

A Better Place

"As the Father has loved me,
so have I loved you.
Abide in my love."
JOHN 15:9 ESV

In John 15, Jesus calls us to remain in his love. It's interesting that the call is to stay in a place of being loved. Why does he need to tell us to stay there? Is it because our propensity is to leave?

God knows man. He created and intricately designed us. If he tells us to remain in his love, it must be possible not to. He knows that when we get busy, understanding that we are loved is one of the first things to go. We have the amazing capacity to do many things *for* him without ever knowing we are loved. Jesus knows this isn't a good place to be.

Are you walking in a place of feeling loved by God? To live without the reality of his love embedded in your heart can produce all sorts of fear and doubt. Receive his invitation today and remain in his love.

Plans for the Future

"I am the way, the truth, and the life.
No one can come to the Father except through me."
JOHN 14:6 NLT

We can rarely see our future clearly. Not knowing what is ahead can feel scary and unsettling, especially when making decisions that concern what's coming next. God tells us that we shouldn't worry. He assures us that he has a plan for us, and a good one at that.

That assurance doesn't only belong to us. Those little ones underfoot that we love so much and spend hours worrying about their futures? God has a plan for them as well. We wonder what type of person they will become, what school they will go to, and who they will marry. God's future for them is better than anything we can plan for them ourselves.

Are you entrusting your children and their futures into God's hands? Rest easy and know that even though you can't map out a step-by-step plan for your future or theirs, God's got both covered.

Tongue Control

*The tongue is a small part of the body yet it carries great power!
Just think of how a small flame can set a huge forest ablaze.
And the tongue is a fire! It can be compared to the sum total of
wickedness and is the most dangerous part of our human body.
It corrupts the entire body and is a hellish flame! It releases a fire
that can burn throughout the course of human existence.*

JAMES 3:5-6 TPT

How many words have you spoken in your life that you wish you could take back? Few things are more convicting or heartbreaking than the first time it happens with our children.

The minute the words leave our mouths, we know we should have held them inside. And we know this because we probably still remember some of the more hurtful words or unsolicited, unhelpful advice offered up by our own parents. It's hard, but it's so important that we get this one right.

In general, do you find it difficult or easy to control your tongue?
In what situations do you find yourself needing restraint with your words?
Ask Jesus to give you the power to speak words that build up,
encourage, and bring light, and for the power to hold your tongue
in the moments those edifying words won't come.

Faithful Servants

"The master said, 'Well done, my good and faithful servant.
You have been faithful in handling this small amount,
so now I will give you many more responsibilities.
Let's celebrate together!'"
MATTHEW 25:23 NLT

As moms, we are women who serve our families, our friends, and our communities. We are faithful in that servitude, praying for strength to get through the required tasks with joy in our hearts. Being faithful means we remain constant and steady in what we have given ourselves to.

Some days constantly supporting our families and other loved ones regardless of circumstance feels exhausting. Firm allegiance in our love and support for them can be tested incredibly. In these moments, we remember God's promise to the faithful. Our service in this life will seem so small when compared to the glory God promises us with him in eternity!

Do you grasp the promise of what is coming? Meditate on that today. God promises us much in our future in return for little right now.

Danger of Discontentment

I am not telling you this because I need anything. I have learned to be satisfied with the things I have and with everything that happens. I know how to live when I am poor, and I know how to live when I have plenty. I have learned the secret of being happy at any time in everything that happens, when I have enough to eat and when I go hungry, when I have more than I need and when I do not have enough.

PHILIPPIANS 4:11-12 NCV

Staying content is a struggle, isn't it? It is a choice to find joy in the place we currently are. Contentment allows us to see beauty in situations that are less than ideal. It keeps us grounded, and it grows a thankful heart.

The danger of discontentment is the temptation for our hearts to wander off of God's course. It allows bitterness to darken the brightest corners of our souls. It tempts us to make decisions that aren't in accordance to God's Word. These decisions can bring trouble and destruction. It's important to be aware of small seeds of discontent trying to take root in our hearts.

Are you finding it hard to be content? God wants you to be content because it protects you from stumbling. He knows how easily your wants and desires can overtake your judgment. Trust him to give you everything you need; then you can be content whether you have little or much!

What Is Required

The LORD has told you what is good,
and this is what he requires of you:
to do what is right, to love mercy,
and to walk humbly with your God.

MICAH 6:8 NLT

As a mother, it feels like there are many things required of us. Sometimes it's hard to tell the essentials from things that are imposed on us by others. The basics are obvious. We need to meet the fundamental needs of our families. But beyond that, what other requirements are before us? Our close relationships legitimately require our *time*.

Does God require something of us too? What makes him happy? We can be encouraged that what God wants of us is much more simple than we think. He's not looking for a supermom. He's looking for a humble mom that boasts in him.

Have you asked the Lord what he requires of you? No flesh will glory in his presence. You don't have to wonder what he wants. He wants your heart.

Byproduct

We know that suffering produces perseverance;
perseverance, character; and character, hope.
ROMANS 5:3-4 NIV

The day we become mothers we realize we'd gladly take any pain this sweet, perfect baby ever encounters onto ourselves. As a result, few things are more tortuous to a mom than watching her child go through trials.

We want to fix it, whatever it is, and make sure our children never, ever have to know the pain of illness, injury, loss, or failure. But we can't. And more importantly, we shouldn't. To let them become the amazing children of God they are meant to be, we have to be willing to let them hurt.

What hurts worse, living through your own pain or watching your child suffer? As painful as it is, hang on to the truth of Romans 5:3-4, and know that whatever they are going through, it is helping them become the people God designed them to be.

Sin Separates

You are not pleased by sacrifices, or I would give them.
You don't want burnt offerings.
The sacrifice God wants is a broken spirit.
God, you will not reject a heart that is broken and sorry for sin.
PSALM 51:16-17 NCV

We all fail and we all sin. Often our sins against those closest to us seem to be more pronounced. We might say or do things to our children that we would never say to a perfect stranger or even a close friend. Close relationships reveal our weaknesses much more clearly. Because we're often with them, we can't escape the proverbial mirror that they frequently hold before our eyes.

God takes our sins seriously because he knows it separates us from him. But he paid the price and suffered punishment on our behalf. He only asks that we repent and turn to him quickly; we don't secure anything but further separation by waiting.

How can you remember that God's love covers a multitude of sins?
He bore all for you so you don't have to. Enjoy the forgiveness that your repentance will usher in. Give him your broken and contrite heart;
he will do the rest.

Calming Waters

Then they cried to the Lord in their trouble,
and he delivered them from their distress.
He made the storm be still,
and the waves of the sea were hushed.
Then they were glad that the waters were quiet,
and he brought them to their desired haven.
PSALM 107:28-30 ESV

When we face trouble, our immediate reaction is to fix the problem. We are geared toward solving issues. However, we are powerless to solve some problems that we face and find ourselves defeated. But we aren't. There is power in calling out to Jesus.

We can go boldly to God with our needs and requests and he will hear us. No problem is bigger than God, and he doesn't consider our requests insignificant. He deeply cares for each of us and will go as far as to calm raging waters for us.

Do you go boldly to God in your time of need? There is such love and comfort in knowing he hears your cries and they aren't ignored.

Worth Holding On

"This is my commandment, that you love one another as I have loved you. Greater love has no one than this, that someone lay down his life for his friends. You are my friends if you do what I command you."
JOHN 15:12-14 ESV

When you find that woman who has been on most of life's journey with you—a sister, a mom, a best friend—hold on to her. When you find that woman who life is easy with—no judgment, shame, or fear of being yourself—hold on to her. When you find that woman you can laugh with, and cry with, all in the same conversation, hold on to her.

Good girlfriends are wonderful to have. They get you when no one else will. They are the people you can go to for advice no matter what time it is. The Bible says that friends encourage and love each other. Those qualities are such a gift, especially when found in that friend that you can do mom life with.

Do you have a friend that blesses your life frequently? Are you that person for someone else? If you have a mutually beneficial friendship, hold onto it. If you don't, start being the kind of friend you need, and see what happens.

Ideal Wardrobe

God has chosen you and made you his holy people. He loves you.
So you should always clothe yourselves with mercy, kindness, humility,
gentleness, and patience. Bear with each other, and forgive each other.
If someone does wrong to you, forgive that person because the Lord
forgave you. Even more than all this, clothe yourself in love. Love is what
holds you all together in perfect unity.
COLOSSIANS 3:12-14 NCV

Did you remember to put on your compassion this morning? Did you slip into your humility, and zip up your discipline?

Not even the cutest boots, most flattering jeans, or perfect shade of lipstick will make us shine as brightly as a mom dressed head-to-toe in love.

What would happen if you consciously applied these attributes the way you apply makeup or choose accessories before you leave your room each day? Ask God which of these your family most needs from you, and let it be the first thing you dress in tomorrow.

A Woman's Closet

She is clothed with strength and dignity;
she can laugh at the days to come.
PROVERBS 31:25 NIV

As women, there are often different clothes we need to wear: the apron for cooking and doing the dishes, the referee shirt for breaking up sibling fights, the scrubs for nursing a sick child, the heels for the fancy work party, and the workout clothes when we're burning off steam at the gym. We wear our pajamas on rainy inside days, and our hats when it has been at least four days since we've had a chance to wash our hair. But one of the most important pieces of clothing we can put on is stated in Proverbs: *strength and dignity.*

Wearing strength can look different for everyone, but we know that strength comes from the Lord. When we feel like we can't even put the shirt over our heads, God will do it for us, giving us the unwavering strength we are praying for.

What pieces of clothing do you wear the most? Do you know that those pieces of clothing are valuable? They are part of the beautiful creature you are as a woman. Whether your closet has only a few pieces in it, or a lot, it is a closet worth cherishing.

A Mother's Comfort

*"As a mother comforts her child,
so I will comfort you."*
ISAIAH 66:13 NIV

When the prophet Isaiah shares God's promises for the restoration of Jerusalem and the church, he invokes the metaphor of a mother. When promising the utmost degree of love and comfort, our Father compares himself to a mother.

Marvel at the gentle power we possess to quiet tears, banish a nightmare, or reassure after an argument with a friend. We are moms. We are the ultimate place of safety and comfort for our children. And when we need that peace and comfort for ourselves, we have God's promise.

It's easy to get wrapped up in being a safety net for others that we forget about ourselves. Where do you go when you need comfort? Is there a nagging worry or concern that you could let go of right now, and let God draw you in his arms instead?

Finding Identity

You are a chosen race, a royal priesthood, a holy nation, a people for his own possession, that you may proclaim the excellencies of him who called you out of darkness into his marvelous light.

1 PETER 2:9 ESV

Upon meeting someone for the first time, one of the first questions we ask is, "What do you do?" In our culture there is great importance placed on who we are and what we do. Moms feel the pressure of defining their identity and measuring up to society's standards. There are hundreds of personality tests to help us determine who we are. These tests, however, are incapable of giving us an accurate description, which is the reason why some of us find ourselves on a continual search to discover who we are.

The answers are closer than we think. They are in Scripture. It doesn't matter how the world perceives us; all that matters is how God sees us.

Who do you let define you?
You are a child of God. You are free. You are chosen.

Sleepless for a Season

I pray that from his glorious, unlimited resources he will empower you with inner strength through his Spirit.

EPHESIANS 3:16 NLT

Are your children still waking up a lot during the night? Sometimes it's not just a hungry baby; it's a feverish child who needs medicine, or a scared toddler that doesn't know why the shadows on their walls are moving. Whatever the reason, often it's a mother's job to interrupt her own precious sleep to care for her children.

When this happens on a regular basis, extreme exhaustion can take place. What we mothers desperately need is sleep, but sometimes it really isn't an option. So, what should we do? The Lord wants us to know that he really will sustain us. It's possible to make an idol out of our missed hours of sleep, constantly counting up the missed hours and almost obsessing over how tired we are.

Take a moment to ask God for his strength. Ask God to help you focus on him and not the sleep you long for. You will find that he has creative ways to energize you, even without sleep. And know that this season isn't forever. It also will pass.

Someone Else

"Pardon your servant, LORD. I have never been eloquent, neither in the past nor since you have spoken to your servant. I am slow of speech and tongue…. Pardon your servant, LORD. Please send someone else."
EXODUS 4:10, 13 NIV

You know those days that have you wondering why God chose you for this life—the ones you wonder what on earth he was thinking because you are so not up to the task? Self-doubt days. You're not alone. In fact, it's one of the oldest themes in the Bible.

Perhaps the most striking example is Moses, a self-proclaimed poor speaker, whom God chose to free the nation of Israel and ultimately deliver the Law to them. When God told Moses to convince the Israelites to follow him, Moses frankly thought he'd made a mistake. Despite God's assurance of success, Moses persisted in his self-doubt.

Have you ever wanted to tell God, "Please send someone else?" Perhaps you are in that very place right now, wondering why God thought you could handle the financial, health, or emotional challenges you are facing as a mother. Instead of giving in to the doubt, share it with your Father. Thank him for his belief in you.

Deep Loss

"Blessed are those who mourn,
for they shall be comforted."
MATTHEW 5:4 ESV

Losing someone we love undeniably leaves a huge hole in the depths of our soul. It constantly aches as a reminder of what we lost. It is a crushing pain, a pain so deep and so fierce it's blinding. In that place of utter darkness, we aren't alone. God aches with us. It's his presence that eases our pain and comforts our broken hearts. He walks with us. He holds us up when grief rips us apart. He never leaves us in our despair.

When the weight of our loss becomes too much for us to carry, he carries it for us.

Are you wrestling with a painful loss? You don't have to mourn alone. Call out to God. He is there. In your sorrow, cling to the one who knows. He loves you more than you can possibly understand.

Swallowed Up

*Say to those with fearful hearts,
"Be strong, and do not fear,
for your God is coming to save you."*
ISAIAH 35:4 NLT

We prepared our children as much as we could for the big, yellow bus that would be coming to swallow them up. *The first trip on the school bus.* We talked to them about how they wouldn't be wearing a seatbelt but that didn't mean they could run around. We taught them about the rules of the bus—older kids sat in the back and younger kids in the front. We made sure they knew their bus number and understood that running anywhere near the bus was not allowed. We coached them up on *everything*.

And then the moment arrived. The bus approached. As we looked down at our children and back at the yellow monster that was lurking, suddenly they looked years younger. We felt the urge to pick them up and run, protecting them from all that would take place in the next thirteen years. We were not ignorant of the dangers facing them in their school years.

When you are faced with letting your children go, can you identify with God watching over you? He would love to pick you up and run away, never letting you endure suffering. But he designed a better plan. Trust in his purpose for you and your children.

No More Fun

*"I am the gate. Those who come in through me will be saved.
They will come and go freely and will find good pastures.
The thief's purpose is to steal and kill and destroy.
My purpose is to give them a rich and satisfying life."*

JOHN 10:9-10 NLT

Whether we grow up knowing and loving Jesus our whole lives and never stray, or whether we come to him later, we all face a time where we wonder if we can follow him and still have fun.

Does loving Christ mean sacrificing our freedom? Particularly with older children, this is a genuine concern. Are we choosing a long list of rules when we choose him? Far from it! This is one of the most beautiful lessons we can share with our kids. A life with Jesus is a life filled with freedom.

Did you know that with the Holy Spirit in your life, you are given free reign? Nothing has any power over you once you give control of your heart to Christ. He will fill you with desire for what he desires. Do you believe this? Spend some time considering how to apply this to your life and how to help your children apply it to theirs.

Never Abandoned

"The LORD himself goes before you and will be with you;
he will never leave you nor forsake you.
Do not be afraid; do not be discouraged."
DEUTERONOMY 31:8 NIV

In a perfect world, every child would have a mother and a father to love and protect them. Families would never be broken. Abandonment would be a stranger to our hearts. Sadly, too many of us know the pain of being left behind, of being forgotten, of being unwanted and discarded as worthless.

These experiences can leave us severely hurt and broken. They might even keep us from pursuing deep relationships. Abandonment causes us to be wary of letting others in. We settle for mediocre relationships in attempt to protect ourselves.

Do you tend to keep God at arm's length? Are you fearful of being hurt? People will fail you, but God will never abandon you. You can trust that his love for you is strong. You are his treasure. He will keep you close. Reach out to him and allow his love to heal those wounds.

After the Heart

All who are being led by the Spirit of God, these are sons of God.
For you have not received a spirit of slavery leading to fear again,
but you have received a spirit of adoption as sons by which we cry out,
"Abba! Father!"
ROMANS 8:14-15 NASB

There is a difference in maturity of faith when we start to see God as our Father instead of just our Creator. We start to discern his voice amidst all the other voices, and we recognize that our actions, thoughts, and lack of trust can leave him yearning for us to be back in his grasp.

As much as we might feel there are other people God desires more or is prouder of because of their spiritual maturity, it is a lie. Sweet daughters of the one true King, he pursues our hearts with abandon. He desires our love. He yearns for the times we speak to him in conversation.

Do you know that God pursues you? Let that thought permeate your being. The Creator of the universe, Abba Father, Alpha and Omega, I Am pursues you. He longs for you to know him. Wherever you are on your spiritual walk, be encouraged that he will not stop pursuing you.

No Choice

*"You didn't choose me. I chose you.
I appointed you to go and produce lasting fruit,
so that the Father will give you whatever you ask for,
using my name."*
JOHN 15:16 NLT

Think of looking into your child's face for the first time. Did you have to decide to love them, or were you overwhelmed immediately by their perfection and innocence? Loving our children is as natural as breathing. We really have no choice, do we? Yet we *do* choose them every day as we care for their needs and nurture their hearts.

Imagine how Jesus' disciples felt as they saw him for the first time, dropped their fishing nets, left their tax collecting businesses, said goodbye to their families—to everything in their known world—and began to follow him around the countryside. Their choice of this homeless, controversy-stirring teacher marked a turning point like no other. Yet just like us with our newborn babies, when faced with his presence and perfection, it really was no choice at all.

Do you remember the day you chose to follow Jesus? Perhaps you were very young when you knew you wanted to walk with him, or possibly this decision was more recent. To choose Jesus is to be chosen by him. Spend some time reflecting on this powerful truth.

Regretful Mother

I call on you, my God, for you will answer me;
turn your ear to me and hear my prayer.
Show me the wonders of your great love.
PSALM 17:6–7 NIV

When we first become mothers, the sky is the limit. We don't know much about the road ahead of us. We just know if things turn out how we would like them to, we will enjoy relationship with our children for the rest of our lives. But sometimes things don't go the way we hope. Sometimes our paths are more full of regret and pain than joyful memories.

Our time is not done yet. Our time of investment and prayer is not over. We mustn't underestimate the power of an interceding mother. This is true even if our children left our homes years ago. God hears our cries.

Does regret dominate your mind? Turn your worry into prayers, and your requests into bold, faith-filled requests. Ask God to increase your faith. Faith is believing what you do not see.

The Sweet Taste

Do not exasperate your children;
instead, bring them up in the training and instruction of the Lord.
EPHESIANS 6:4 NIV

There are little tidbits of fruit that moms of young children are able to witness. They come in the most unexpected moments. When we hear our four-year-old ask the waitress for chocolate milk with please and thank you, when we hear joyous laughter between our toddler and three-year-old, or when our kindergartner is walking out to the bus and reminds us that we didn't pray at breakfast but he knows he can just pray in his mind.

Maybe when we're at church taking communion our daughter says, "I want that, Momma; I want Jesus to live in my heart." We begin to think they are really getting it. These are moments to celebrate.

Have you seen fruit for your labor in your kids yet? Think on them. Keep encouraging your children in their walk, keep nurturing their precious spirits, keep loving them as Christ loves you. They might just be moments but thank God for them. The glory is his.

Keeping an Account

*There is therefore now no condemnation
for those who are in Christ Jesus.*
ROMANS 8:1 ESV

Mothers are known to have all sorts of skill sets and abilities. We can manage our households, bandage a scraped knee, change a flat tire, comfort away fears, and make an amazing dinner. Do you know what else we are really good at? Carrying shame and guilt.

How many sleepless nights are spent feeling heavy, recounting everything we didn't do, or wished we had done better? We easily become slaves to our own regrets: regrets that inhibit us from growing into the mothers God intends us to be. We don't need to be discouraged. We are broken. We make mistakes. But God is so gracious. When we are faced with failure, let us be quick to seek his forgiveness and accept his grace.

Do you keep an account of your shortcomings? God wants to bring you out of a place of self-condemnation and into a place of freedom. It's by accepting his grace that you can live a victorious life. Let your shame and guilt go today and be free.

August

God gave us a spirit not of fear
but of power and love and self-control.

2 Timothy 1:7 esv

Individually Designed

My frame was not hidden from you
when I was made in the secret place,
when I was woven together in the depths of the earth.
Your eyes saw my unformed body;
all the days ordained for me were written in your book
before one of them came to be.
PSALM 139:15-16 NIV

Do you remember the first time your child surprised you? Few things are more delightful than watching our little babies become little people. Personalities emerge, opinions form, and what God has known all along begins to unfold.

In this light, parenting can be seen as a long process of becoming acquainted with our children. What a gift! They will be both like us and entirely unique, and we must strive to embrace both. They got our dimples, but not our love of music. Their eyes are just like ours, and so is their need to always be right. They are ours to nurture and love, but first, last, and always, they are *his*.

What fascinates you about your children?
What delights you?
What are you learning about who God has designed them to be?

Wealth of Wisdom

*If any of you lacks wisdom, you should ask God,
who gives generously to all without finding fault,
and it will be given to you.*

JAMES 1:5 NIV

Motherhood encompasses so many things. It is filled with so much joy and many blessings. However, it is undeniably a huge undertaking that is both physically and emotionally taxing. The world is quick to tell us how-to and how-not-to parent, but essentially we enter into the role of motherhood without a manual or a clear instruction guide. It is impossible to prepare for every unique parenting challenge that may come our way.

Yet we need not fear. God is the perfect parent and teacher. His wisdom is ours for the taking. All we have to do is ask him. In every situation, in every decision made, we are not without help.

You don't have to depend on your minimal experience; you can rely on God's infinite knowledge. What parenting questions do you want to ask him today?

Stewarding the Mind

If people's thinking is controlled by the sinful self, there is death.
But if their thinking is controlled by the Spirit, there is life and peace.
ROMANS 8:6 NCV

One of the best disciplines we moms can practice is to be good stewards of our minds. Many thoughts will pass through our minds during the course of a day. Some are inconsequential. But there are plenty of other thoughts as well. Some come from God, some come from the enemy, and some come from outside sources. We need to be good stewards of what we allow to stay in our minds and protect what we put before our eyes and ears in the first place!

If our minds are set on the flesh and on worldly thinking, Jesus says this will ultimately lead to death. However, setting our minds on the Spirit is life and peace. Often our circumstances aren't what need to change; it's our mind and how we steward our thoughts.

Are your thoughts leading you to fear, anxiety, and worry?
Set your mind on the Spirit. It will be life and peace to you.

City without Walls

The grace of God has appeared that offers salvation to all people.
It teaches us to say "No" to ungodliness and worldly passions,
and to live self-controlled, upright and godly lives in this present age.
TITUS 2:11-12 NIV

In grade school, we had to wait to speak until our hand was raised. The teacher would not call on a single student until she had finished talking. The children could barely wait another second before blurting out the answer. These teachers were wise. They were trying to teach self-control, a valuable life lesson.

Lack of self-control comes in a variety of forms: overeating, spending too much time on the computer or phone, losing our tempers, wasting money, gossiping, and the list goes on. Self-control is an area that requires discipline. In order to perfect it, we need to practice and ask God for help. Proverbs 25:28 describes a man without self-control as a city broken into and left without walls. What an easy way to let the enemy in.

Which areas in your life require you to practice more self-control?
Who can you be accountable to?
Ask for help today in the area of self-control.
Bring your weakness into the light and find the help you need in the Lord.

The Protector

"When you pass through the waters, I will be with you;
and when you pass through the rivers,
they will not sweep over you.
When you walk through the fire, you will not be burned;
the flames will not set you ablaze."

ISAIAH 43:2 NIV

From the first time someone else holds our precious new babies, our thoughts fix on their safety. *Is she using both hands?* Remember that first car trip? How many times did you look back at your (probably sleeping) baby? Were you leaning back as you drove, one hand on the car seat, making sure no turn was too sharp or stop too sudden?

God feels that same way about our children and about us. There is nothing he won't do to protect his children. He is right there even when we can't be. Go ahead and drive with both hands; he's got this.

Is it comfortable and natural for you to entrust your children to others, or do you struggle to let go? How about with God? Share your heart with him; ask him to strengthen your confidence and thank him for how very much he loves you and your children.

Rest for the Weary

"Come to me, all of you who are weary and carry heavy burdens, and I will give you rest. Take my yoke upon you. Let me teach you, because I am humble and gentle at heart, and you will find rest for your souls."

MATTHEW 11:28-29 NLT

Can you remember the last time you were alone? I mean really alone. Free from any demands and distractions in a quiet cozy corner of your own to breathe deeply? It is difficult to function well when our hearts and minds are full of noise and chaos. The only way we can possibly operate is to give space for quiet and peace to make a home deep within us.

Stealing away for some peaceful moments is vital to being a good mom. We get so busy taking care of others that we often forget to take care of ourselves.

Do you feel fatigued? Making time with the Lord so he can recharge you is a wonderful gift you can give to your children. Schedule it into your day guilt free.

Season of Waiting

In their hearts humans plan their course,
but the LORD establishes their steps.
PROVERBS 16:9 NIV

Being in a season of waiting can be trying. When our flesh desires the next thing, and God has a different plan, we might feel our trust waver in weakness. We might cry out in frustration or get angry at the tiniest of things. Our flesh can be our biggest adversary. It has desires that are ungodly, wants that are unnecessary, and longings that just aren't right for us. This is where faith comes in.

Believing in something we can't see isn't for the faint of heart. It takes prayer, a listening ear, and trust. There is a beautiful gift to unwavering trust in God; we can give up control because there is nothing we can do anyway. There is no point in frantically worrying because he has decided for us. He will gladly take that burden from us.

Do you have an unwavering trust in God that he has determined your life plan? Trusting in a God who loves you unconditionally and has your best interests at the forefront of his mind is an incredible place to rest.

Isolation

Christ will make his home in your hearts as you trust in him. Your roots will grow down into God's love and keep you strong. And may you have the power to understand, as all God's people should, how wide, how long, how high, and how deep his love is. May you experience the love of Christ, though it is too great to understand fully.

EPHESIANS 3:17-19 NLT

In the depths of motherhood, it is easy to feel isolated from the rest of the world especially when days are more hard than easy.

We are not alone. He is there when we rock our babies in the early morning light, groggy without sleep. He sees us slaving over the stove with a toddler fussing at our feet and a baby on our hip. He surrounds us when we are anxious over a feverish child. He is with us as we wait for our teenagers to come home after curfew. God knows every worry and thought. And every sacrifice given.

Do you feel alone today? Remember that everything you do is accounted for: God sees every kiss, every hug, every extra bedtime story read, every sleepless night and early morning. You are not alone. Ask God to make his presence known to you.

Supported by Love

When I said, "My foot is slipping,"
your unfailing love, Lord, supported me.
PSALM 94:18 NIV

As moms, we practice giving copious amounts of love away. In the early years we are in the season of pouring our love on our children daily. This includes long hours in the morning when our muscles burn from holding an infant, long hours in the afternoon reading repetitive books, and long hours in the night when we are awakened by lonely, sick, hungry, or scared children.

We do it because we love them. We do it because love, by its very definition, lays its life down for others. But on many days, our love tanks run dry. We feel hungry, lonely, or sick. When we go into the bathroom to steal ninety seconds of quiet, it's imperative that we go to our good Father and ask him to fill us by pouring his love back into us. And he will.

Do you need your love tank filled?
You will never be found in want when you ask.

Giving Up Control

You can make many plans,
but the LORD's purpose will prevail.
PROVERBS 19:21 NLT

We are made to be different, but we all fit into categories with certain areas of our life: some are worriers, some are romantics, some are planners, and some are controllers. Some of us cannot give up control of the little things or the big things. We like to know exactly what is going to happen, when, and how. We want to know where our children will be at all hours of the day. We have massive calendars with every half-hour detailed out. We balance our checkbooks to the cent. We have our ten-year life plan. And then it happens: an unexpected occurrence.

What do we do then? There isn't much we can do besides letting it go. We can release the burden of misunderstanding to God. We can have unwavering trust in the Father who loves us. There is someone at work in us who knows us best and has a specific purpose for our lives.

Have you had an unexpected life event where unwavering trust in God was your only option? How did that prepare your heart for future events that were out of your control?

Just Be There

Then they sat on the ground with him for seven days and seven nights. No one said a word to him, because they saw how great his suffering was.
JOB 2:13 NIV

As a mother, few things hurt more than seeing our children suffer. We want to take away their pain, to tell them better days are coming. When they are little, this can often be done. The skinned knees and broken toys of childhood lead inevitably to bigger problems, problems we can't always solve.

The more mature and independent these beings we are blessed to love and nurture become, the harder it becomes to know what to do or even to say when they are hurting. Maybe that's ok. Maybe just our presence is enough.

Do you struggle with wanting to fix everything for your children?
How do you handle it when you can't?
As the story of Job continues, his friends turn to that strategy with disastrous effect. Ask God to show you when just your presence, your love, and prayers are all your children need from you.

Mothers Unite

A person standing alone can be attacked and defeated,
but two can stand back-to-back and conquer.
Three are even better, for a triple-braided cord is not easily broken.
ECCLESIASTES 4:12 NLT

When we look at all the other moms around us, we often think that they
have it all together. Their lives, homes, and marriages are perfect. We
imagine that they don't struggle with the same issues we do. They are
strong and confident. We begin to question what is wrong with us. Why
are we so needy? Why do we feel so incompetent and alone?

The truth is that every mother struggles with the same feelings of
loneliness and inadequacy. Chances are, they are looking at you and
wondering how you have it all together! We need each other for support
and encouragement. We need each other to celebrate life's ups and
downs. There is comfort in knowing that we are in this journey together.

Who are the mothers in your life?
You are not alone. There is always a mother nearby. Fight the temptation
to appear perfect and let your fellow mothers into your reality. Standing
together only makes you stronger. Battle together, love together, do life
together. Be real in your joys and struggles.

Compassion in Loss

"To strengthen those crushed by despair who mourn in Zion—
to give them a beautiful bouquet in the place of ashes,
the oil of bliss instead of tears,
and the mantle of joyous praise
instead of the spirit of heaviness.
Because of this, they will be known as
Mighty Oaks of Righteousness,
planted by Yahweh as a living display of his glory."
ISAIAH 61:3 TPT

This is for all the moms who lost a baby before it had a chance to enter the world. It can feel like that tragedy is written on our foreheads. Like we'll walk into the nearby coffee shop and when heads turn to see who walked in, they will know. They'll know the suffering we are enduring. They'll know that just a few weeks ago we were the happiest we could be, excited about the possibility of welcoming a little one into the world. And then it happened.

Many try to comfort with similar stories, but we still feel alone. We feel like no one can possibly understand what we are going through. Sweet friends, someone does understand, and he loves us like no other. He is holding our babies in his arms and sitting next to us stroking our heads in compassion.

Have you lost a baby? God has not left you. He wants to lead you into his light and flood your soul with peace. He will demonstrate his compassion and understanding during your grieving process. Cry out to him.

Stuck in Sin

If we are faithless, he remains faithful,
for he cannot disown himself.

2 TIMOTHY 2:13 NIV

Have you ever felt stuck in a certain behavior or sin? Is there something that seems to weigh you down? These are the things the devil uses to discourage us. He knows that discouragement does more damage than the actual sin. When we are discouraged, we continue to sin.

This is when we most need to contend for our freedom and breakthrough. We confess our sin to him, and we receive his forgiveness. He will be faithful to forgive us again and again. When we feel God's authentic forgiveness, it increases our strength to resist the sin next time.

Are you struggling with sin? Jesus says in your struggle, look to him; he is the author and perfector of your faith (Hebrews 12:1-2). You are not. Lean mightily on his ability to complete that which he began.

Loving Enemies

*"I say, love your enemies!
Pray for those who persecute you!"*

MATTHEW 5:44 NLT

Love your enemy. We've all heard it, but how do we live it? It's a baffling command; an enemy is defined as someone actively opposed to you. How will you help your children when it comes time for them to face— and to love—someone who wants to see them fail?

To show love to someone engaged in trying to topple us requires superhuman strength. Do we have superhuman strength? Do our children? None of us does, yet Jesus tells us we must. He wants us to be set apart, so others will know he lives in us. We must rely on the Holy Spirit, move out of the way, and let his love rule our hearts.

What might the world look like if all God's children spent a portion of their day praying for anyone who might wish them harm? What would the world see in you, or in your kids, if you chose to live this way? Share your thoughts on this with God.

Mentorship

Older women can teach the young women to love their husbands,
to love their children, to be wise and pure,
to be good workers at home, to be kind.
TITUS 2:4-5 NCV

Most expectant mothers in our culture are thrown a baby shower. Along with gifts of diapers, toys, and clothes, they are also handed a ton of advice from seasoned mothers.

"It takes a village to raise a child." This is such a true expression. Sometimes we don't have all the answers, but there is always a mom who has walked this road ahead of us. That experience gives her wisdom and perspective from a road already traveled. Instead of determining to figure it all out on our own, it is good to ask questions and glean wisdom from others. They are our God-given village.

Who in your life can you glean wisdom and learning from?
Seek these women out. They are eager to lend a hand and lighten your load. Embrace them, cry on their shoulders, and appreciate their compassionate hearts. They are a wonderful gift to all who are willing to accept help and learn.

In Need of Energy

He gives strength to the weary and increases the power of the weak.
Even youths grow tired and weary, and young men stumble and fall;
but those who hope in the LORD will renew their strength.
They will soar on wings like eagles; they will run and not grow weary,
they will walk and not be faint.

ISAIAH 40:29-31 NIV

Picture a pregnant mom, desperate for a nap, hopelessly watching her two-year-old climb out of bed (again) and head for the toy bin. "No nap, Mama. I not tired!" Now envision the gorgeous mother with the impeccably dressed triplets. "I wonder how she does it," we say to one another. "I sure wish I had that kind of energy!"

Have you ever met a mom who *hasn't* wished for more energy? Kids are exhausting; *life* is exhausting! How wonderful that we have a God who supplies us with all we need.

As you look at the mountain of responsibility before you, don't be afraid to tell God you're tired. He wants to give you the strength not just to finish but to soar. Thank him for ensuring you will always have enough energy to fulfill his purpose.

Younger Years

People ought to enjoy every day of their lives,
no matter how long they live.
ECCLESIASTES 11:8 NCV

When your children are little, the days seem to go by painfully slowly. It is easy to look at mothers with older children and be envious. They look wide-awake, showered, and calm. You smell of peanut-butter and jelly and can't remember if you did your hair today or yesterday for that matter.

If we stare at all we can't do and all seems lost, we will miss the treasures of the younger years. There will be a day when our children cannot fit in our laps, when we are not needed to help them get dressed, when they are capable of making all their meals. When those days arrive, our season of demonstrating intense sacrificial love is gone.

Can you take joy in the younger years? Those moms who look wide-awake, showered, and calm? They were in your position not so long ago. In just a few years, that will be you.

Intentionally Present

This is the day the LORD has made;
We will rejoice and be glad in it.
PSALM 118:24 NKJV

Life is a blur especially when we have little ones underfoot. It is only natural for us to dream about what is to come. We ponder a new move, a new job, an addition to the family. We find ourselves saying, "When she is older, I'll be less tired," or "When I get promoted, my finances will get back on track," or "When the spring comes, I'll go back to the gym." And so the cycle continues.

God's blessings are in the here and now. Tomorrow will come soon enough. How would our perspective of life change if we chose to be intentional about being present in each day? Would we make better decisions? Would we become more aware of the gifts God has already given us? Would we invest more into the relationships around us? If we always seek after what is to come, even good things, we will lose sight of what we already have. We lose the ability to soak in life around us.

Are you always looking ahead? Stop what you are doing and enjoy the moment you are in. Fully appreciate and live in the present. In what ways can you slow down and appreciate the now?

Mom Advice

The wise woman builds her house,
But the foolish pulls it down with her hands.
PROVERBS 14:1 NKJV

It is easy to make our children feel disrespected. Their actions and attitudes bother us, so we start to challenge them on everything they say and do. It is hard to avoid because we want our children to be successful in life. We think we're helping them by heaping on the mom advice. But that advice isn't always wanted, and it can lead us down a path of nagging and belittlement.

We need to accept that our children are in the process of learning. This means we choose to build them up with encouragement instead of tearing them down when they make mistakes. And they *will* make mistakes. All the mom advice in the world isn't going to stop our children from failing, and it might be more hurtful than helpful sometimes. Instead, we should be there to pick them up when they do fail, and lovingly teach them how to be successful next time.

What is one tangible way you can encourage or build your children up today? If you choose to encourage your children when they fail, they will be more receptive to your advice next time. In fact, they might even seek you out for it.

The Family

Jesus looked at him and said, "Let me introduce you to my true mother and brothers." Then gesturing to the disciples gathered around him, he said, "Look closely, for this is my true family. When you obey my heavenly Father, that makes you a part of my true family."

MATTHEW 12:48-50 TPT

You may come from a traditional family or a pieced-together family. You may have been adopted, abandoned, or put through the foster system. Whatever your story, when you accepted Jesus Christ into your life as your Lord and Savior, you were welcomed into one big, happy family. Isn't that a beautiful picture? People gathered together, doing the will of God, rejoicing in togetherness for one purpose—to glorify God.

Whatever your life story up to the point of accepting Jesus, let it be your past and not your present or your future. If you were lost, you are found in Christ. If you were broken, you are being put back together. If you were a mess, you are being pruned and reshaped. If you were alone, you are surrounded by a body of believers.

What was your family like before you became a believer?
What is your new family like? Does it give you peace to know you are accepted into the family of Christ?

Power Made Perfect

"My grace is enough for you. When you are weak, my power is made perfect in you." So I am very happy to brag about my weaknesses. Then Christ's power can live in me. For this reason I am happy when I have weaknesses, insults, hard times, sufferings, and all kinds of troubles for Christ. Because when I am weak, then I am truly strong.

2 CORINTHIANS 12:9-10 NCV

It's one of those days. One more straw and your back will surely break. It's tempting to give in to tears and frustration, but the apostle Paul offers another approach. Rejoice! Suffering is a gift! Wait. What?

Paul reminds us that Christ's power can really only show itself when we are at our weakest. It's a game changer, seeing the trifecta of a broken dishwasher, vomiting child, and near-impossible work deadline as a gift. We really can't handle it all, but we have someone who can.

Are you trying to do it all and then some? Feeling overwhelmed and under-equipped? Wonderful! It's the perfect time to surrender your weakness to the awesome power of God.

Just Rest

The LORD will give strength to His people;
The LORD will bless His people with peace.
PSALM 29:11 NKJV

Picture a season in your life where you were knee-deep in busyness, swallowed in sadness, or buried in exhaustion. Picture that season and how you looked, how you acted, how you reacted, how you survived. Now picture Jesus. See his face, feel his warmth, envision his smile. Picture yourself back in that same tiresome season, sitting on a chair in your house, desiring to spend time with God but being so extremely tired that you couldn't find the strength. So you sit.

Here comes Jesus walking toward you. You invite him to come closer but are ready with the excuses and reasons for why you have been absent from him. He walks toward you and outstretches his hand. When he reaches you, his hand starts to move toward your head. Gently, ever so lovingly, he pushes your head to the chair back, and whispers, "Rest, Daughter, just rest."

Have you encountered a moment with Jesus where you understood more fully that he gets you to your very core? He knows your heart. He knows when your soul needs rest. Let him stroke your hair and sing you a lullaby.

Making a Home

She speaks wise words
and teaches others to be kind.
She watches over her family
and never wastes her time.
Her children speak well of her.
PROVERBS 31:26-28 NCV

Women love to create homes; just check out Pinterest, Instagram, or any other social networking site. There are thousands of do-it-yourself home projects and décor ideas. But making a home is much more than cute furniture and pretty paint colors. We have the ability to create a dwelling place full of warmth and laughter. We can provide a place for our family to live where there is rest, security, and comfort.

It's good to reflect on what type of home we desire our children to grow up in. Don't we want a home where our children's spiritual foundation is strongly built?

What type of home are you building for your children? Aim to make it an escape from the busy world, a place where God's Word is heard and loved, and a place they can freely gather to share and pray for each other. Make it a home with God at the center.

What God Wants

I have not kept the good news of your justice hidden in my heart;
I have talked about your faithfulness and saving power.
I have told everyone in the great assembly
of your unfailing love and faithfulness.
PSALM 40:10 NLT

Even before we acquire language, we can tell when we have done something good. Babies see our delighted reaction to their first smiles, giggles, and coos, and they smile, giggle, and coo some more. It makes them happy to bring us happiness. Seeing their joy brings us joy, so we heap even more laughter and smiles on them.

Praise and recognition are basic human desires given to us by God, and he desires the same. More than any great deed or accomplishment, he wants to hear our praise and receive our thanks. As a proud and loving Father, it brings him great joy to bring us joy.

How do your children react when you praise them? How do you respond when they recognize all you do for them? Magnify that happiness as far as you can, and you might get an inkling of how God feels when you praise his name and share what he has done for you.

The Copycat

Imitate God, therefore, in everything you do, because you are his dear children. Live a life filled with love, following the example of Christ. He loved us and offered himself as a sacrifice for us, a pleasing aroma to God.

EPHESIANS 4:32-5:2 NLT

Our children watch everything we do. It is always fun when the one-year-old starts walking around with her hand up to her ear like she's on the phone, or nodding his head and laughing out loud like he's seen his mother do, or sitting by an older child trying to put on her shoes too. At one, imitation is essential. The actions copied during this stage of life have significance. Isn't it amazing that God created us this way?

In Ephesians, we are called to be imitators of God. That's a very lofty goal. But Ephesians goes on to say we are God's children. To imitate God, we have to understand that he does everything in love. He deals with us in compassion, grace, and forgiveness. We, in turn, are to treat others the same way.

What does imitating God mean to you? If a one-year-old understands that his or her actions have significance, you have the ability to grasp that and ask God to help you as well.

Life Seasons

He has made everything beautiful in its time.
He has also set eternity in the human heart;
yet no one can fathom what God has done from beginning to end.
I know that there is nothing better for people
than to be happy and to do good while they live.
ECCLESIASTES 3:11-12 NIV

Are you trying to do too much? Do you even know? Success lies in knowing the season of life that we are in. As long as we know what the parameters of our seasons are, we won't try to do things that are specific to other seasons.

Are our children sick? Then for today, our *season* is nursing our children back to health. Knowing *that* is our season can relieve us of the burden of caring for others today. Maybe we're trying to focus on neglected relationships. Then this season may be one of nurturing our relationships back to health, and not volunteering for another charity event.

Can you identify which season you are in today? Think of the things that need to be done specific to that season. Ask God to give you strength in each season and to help you be aware of which season you are in.

No Shame

"I—yes, I alone—will blot out your sins for my own sake
and will never think of them again."

ISAIAH 43:25 NLT

There is beauty in admitting where we were before we knew Jesus Christ. So often we want to keep it a secret. Honesty allows God to mold us and shape us into the people he wants us to be: free from the condemnation of the past. There is freedom and empowerment in declaring, "I once was lost, but now I am found!"

We can be proud to acknowledge the work God has done in our life. Our testimonies are a powerful witness. We shouldn't be ashamed of our history. Our stories may bring comfort to those who feel alone and lost or encourage others to look at their own lives and see their need for grace and forgiveness.

Do you feel ashamed of who you were before you became a Christian? Shrug off the shame, and boldly proclaim the work Jesus Christ has done in you. You could change the course of someone's life forever.

The Game of Life

When I am afraid,
I will put my trust in you.
I praise God for what he has promised.
I trust in God, so why should I be afraid?
PSALM 56:3-4 NLT

Do you remember the Game of Life? You start by picking the color car you want. Then the game simulated your travels through life, from college to retirement, with jobs, marriage, and blue or pink pegs that fit in your car representing your children. The game was a way to picture your ideal life, and the possibilities were endless. Inevitably, the game was set up to chance, and you could lose family members, become bankrupt, or be forced to change careers if certain cards were drawn.

Often we are traveling down the walk of life, happy and content. Then the chance card is drawn. Suddenly our perfect utopia is disrupted by unshakeable circumstances that make us question everything we know to be true. In those moments, we must remember that Jesus is no stranger to pain, loss, or heartache. In those moments, we don't worry about whether we're growing in maturity of faith, or if we're responding the right way; we just ask for his comfort.

Have you experienced an unshakeable circumstance?
Jesus' comfort is the best thing for your heart in times of strife.
He understands your heartache.

Living with Worry

Don't worry about anything; instead, pray about everything.
Tell God what you need, and thank him for all he has done. Then you will
experience God's peace, which exceeds anything we can understand.
His peace will guard your hearts and minds as you live in Christ Jesus.
PHILIPPIANS 4:6-7 NLT

Living with children means living with worry. It's true, isn't it? They run ahead of you in a parking lot, and you worry. They take their first jump into the deep end, and you worry. The list goes on and on.

Expecting perfect calm when our babies encounter danger is unrealistic, but allowing that normal, human response to control us and to steal our peace is unnecessary. The moment the feeling arises, we can take a breath, remember how much God loves us, and pray. He promises to bring us peace.

As you read this, what worries came to mind? Try Paul's advice out right now. Open your heart to God; share your concerns with him and see how he comes in to guard your heart.

Slow to Anger

Everyone should be quick to listen,
slow to speak and slow to become angry,
because human anger does not produce
the righteousness that God desires.
JAMES 1:19–20 NIV

God is slow to anger. This phrase is repeated numerous times in the Old Testament and referenced in the New Testament. God wants us to know it! He also wants us to see that he has demonstrated it time and time again throughout all creation.

It takes a long time to make God angry. His anger isn't impulsive. Furthermore, it is rightly directed. The subjects of God's anger are often people or nations that have hurt his people. When God finally does express his anger, it is always just. It is wonderful to know our God isn't impulsive or explosive. He is a stable, safe Father.

Take some time to study where God says he is slow to anger. Don't berate yourself for your angry outbursts. Confess them to him (and others when needed), receive his forgiveness, and enjoy the fact that he will never be quick to anger with you.

September

All Scripture is inspired by God
and profitable for teaching,
for reproof, for correction,
for training in righteousness.

2 Timothy 3:16 nasb

Priority of Presence

"Don't worry about tomorrow,
because tomorrow will have its own worries.
Each day has enough trouble of its own."
MATTHEW 6:34 NCV

Do you remember how slow time could pass when we were children? It was pure agony waiting for a special holiday or fun event to arrive. Now as adults, life tends to rush by. Days blend into weeks, and weeks into months. Trying to manage it all and stay present in each moment is not an easy task.

We become tired and worn down from the same routine every day. Discouragement and restlessness can overtake even the most devoted of mothers. However, defining our purpose and taking possession of our days makes every day meaningful. The dishes will always be there, as will the laundry, but those things don't really matter.

Are you able to stay present in each moment? The deep and lasting impact of your presence does have significance in your child's life. Make being present a priority.

Take a Picture

Whoever is slow to anger has great understanding,
but one who has a hasty temper exalts folly.
PROVERBS 14:29 NRSV

We may all have been shocked by our children's ability to destroy our houses. It's amazing what they can do in a matter of minutes. Sometimes we find their messes cute, almost charming. We tell ourselves that the vase they broke wasn't really expensive, the stained carpet needed replacing anyway, or the lost earring wasn't very special. In those moments, it's easy to laugh off their antics.

But what about when they *do* destroy something special or irreplaceable? When we are first accosted with their destruction, it's important not to respond impulsively. If we can take two minutes and calm ourselves down, we will have a much more godly response. Everything we have is just stuff. We won't take it with us when we leave this earth. Our responses shape how our children view failure.

The next time you have to take two minutes before responding, grab your camera. Take a picture of your child sitting in the flour on the kitchen floor, pointing to their masterpiece on the wall, or leaning against the car with the dented door. It will lighten your heart and give you all a great memory to share in the years to come.

Iron and Iron

As iron sharpens iron,
so one person sharpens another.
PROVERBS 27:17 NIV

Have you ever found a friend later in life that surprised you? A girlfriend, maybe, who you met at church one morning and bonded with instantly? After several more coffee chats, you and this friend feel more like sisters than friends. You can't imagine how you ever got along in life without her. She is similar to you, which makes conversation easy, but your differences are also obvious. These girlfriends can be hard to find.

We often look to be friends with people who are similar to us. Friendships take work; they aren't always natural. They require us to go deeper than we like, showing how vulnerable and real we can be with others. When you rub two blades together, the edges become sharper, making those blades more efficient. As friends, we are meant to share, to hold accountable, to encourage, to pray for, to *sharpen* each other.

Do you have someone in your life who helps sharpen you?
Can you see that the sharpening process is beneficial to both of you?
You need friends who are willing to ask the hard questions,
and you can be that friend right back.

Seeking Praise

"When you give to someone in need, don't do as the hypocrites do—blowing trumpets in the synagogues and streets to call attention to their acts of charity! I tell you the truth, they have received all the reward they will ever get."

MATTHEW 6:2 NLT

"Mommy, look what I did!" Kids love praise, and they learn early on who to get it from. "That's the most beautiful flower drawing I've ever seen!" we gush.

We love to be recognized; it's human nature. It feels good to be complimented for the countless hours we spent organizing the school fundraiser, caring for a sick friend's child, or volunteering to help the poor. We feel seen and validated. There's nothing wrong with this as long as our motive remains to give love freely. However, if we discover we are performing these seemingly selfless acts in order to gain the approval of others, it's time to take a step back.

When you give your time, resources, or attention to something, do you examine your heart? If you are reacting to pressure, hoping to impress someone, or outright seeking attention, go straight to God with your honest feelings. Ask him to fill you with a desire to please only him, so your children will have an example to model their own actions on.

Vision Statement

Since, then, you have been raised with Christ,
set your hearts on things above,
where Christ is, seated at the right hand of God.
Set your minds on things above, not on earthly things.
COLOSSIANS 3:1-2 NIV

Most successful businesses have a vision statement that outlines their purpose and goals. It not only helps motivate the workplace, it also keeps the business focused on the end goal. Anything that doesn't align with that statement or prohibits the end goal is disregarded.

As busy moms, what is our vision statement for our families? It is good to have one. What fills our schedules and steals our time? We need to reclaim our families by saying no to unnecessary distractions that pull us away from our vision statement.

What is your vision statement for your family?
What things distract you from it?

Passing On Faith

I am reminded of your sincere faith, which first lived in your grandmother Lois and in your mother Eunice and, I am persuaded, now lives in you also.
2 TIMOTHY 1:5 NIV

Paul loved Timothy for many reasons, and chief among them was his devotion to Jesus. Timothy was a young man, but he had influences throughout his life, inspiring and helping to form his faith.

Even if we didn't grow up in a faith-filled household, we can start a legacy today, with our own children, by sharing the light inside us every chance we get.

Do your children see you living out your faith?
What things, both big and small, could you do to help
ensure the faith you have will live in your children?

Skip for Joy

The LORD says, "Forget what happened before,
and do not think about the past.
Look at the new thing I am going to do.
It is already happening. Don't you see it?
I will make a road in the desert
and rivers in the dry land."
ISAIAH 43:18-19 NCV

One of the best promises Jesus makes when we accept him as our Lord and Savior is a new start. A rebirth. A chance to wipe our dirty slate clean. This acceptance of our past, no matter what the circumstance, should be enough to make us want to skip down the sidewalk in joy. We've been given a second chance. We are made new in the name of Jesus Christ.

If we are holding on to something from twenty years ago, we are free to let it go. If the shame and hurt from that moment in our past has been stopping us from living in joy, we can be redeemed through Jesus. In his name, we are reborn and set free. The chains are broken. We can kick them off and start skipping!

Are you letting something from years ago define the rest of your life? The enemy has taken enough from you; don't let him have one day more. Instead, ask Jesus to make you new and believe in the depths of your heart that he stands firm in his promise to you.

Differing Advice

"Anyone who hears my teaching and doesn't obey it is foolish, like a person who builds a house on sand. When the rains and floods come and the winds beat against that house, it will collapse with a mighty crash."
MATTHEW 7:26-27 NLT

If you are looking for mommy advice, there is a plethora of resources. Just Google *"how to be a good mom,"* and you will be bombarded with millions of extensively written articles. Most people are eager to tell you how to parent without you even asking. From well-intentioned friends, to childcare providers and health professionals, everyone has an opinion on the most effective ways to parent.

All the advice and opinions can be overwhelming. However, the way God defines good parenting is not the way the world defines it. Looking to the world to model parenthood is confusing. Instead, we need to look directly to Jesus for advice. Know him and you will know the Father's heart.

Who are you looking to for parenting advice?
Modeling your parenting style after Jesus is the best way to parent.
Take the time to study his Word; research his attributes and qualities
shown within. Look to him for advice and guidance.

Taught to Pray

My child, pay attention to what I say.
Listen carefully to my words.
Don't lose sight of them.
Let them penetrate deep into your heart,
for they bring life to those who find them,
and healing to their whole body.
PROVERBS 4:20–22 NLT

One of the most important conversations our children will ever have begins when they are little. It's the on-going dynamic conversation between them and their Maker, otherwise known as *prayer*. While it is personal, we can do things that help our children turn to God in prayer. We can model for our children our own prayer lives. When we are grateful, we can thank God in front of them. When we don't know what to do, we can ask him for help in their presence.

When our children are little, we might give them the opportunity to repeat after us as they are learning to pray. As they get older, we can switch to coaching them in their own prayers. It is ultimately a relationship we are aiming to foster, not a checklist they need to complete.

Are you teaching your children to pray? As they realize the ease with which prayer comes, you won't have to do much more than listen. When they personally grasp his amazing love, they will be drawn back again and again.

Simple Encouragement

Be on your guard;
stand firm in the faith;
be courageous; be strong.
Do everything in love.
1 CORINTHIANS 16:13-14 NIV

Kids leave. They grow up, stop being kids, and they leave. We hope we've told them everything they need to hear, and that they've really *heard* it. They'll be faced with many tests of their values and challenges to their faith. They will make choices entirely on their own; all we can do is pray and hope they make the right ones.

In his closing remarks to the Corinthians, Paul leaves them with these short, simple encouragements intended to help them hold onto their faith without his guidance.

Where can you place these powerful verses so your child will see them? How can you make this part of your family culture? Consider each of Paul's admonishments. What does it mean to be on guard, stand firm, and be courageous and strong? What does it look like to do everything in love?

Blessed in Mourning

Weeping may last through the night,
but joy comes with the morning.
PSALM 30:5 NLT

There can be many sources of grief. There may have been a death, or maybe it was the loss of something else: a job, a dream, a friendship. Grief seems to come without warning or invitation. It takes over our homes and lives in almost every facet.

It is critical during this season that we let the Lord lead us. He asks nothing more than for us to lie in his strong arms. As we lay there, he will faithfully whisper words of comfort. When we're in this state of grief, he calls us *blessed*. That's right. Read Matthew 5:4. He calls us blessed because he knows he is going to pour a measure of comfort over us that we wouldn't receive otherwise. That comfort will sustain us when it seems nothing else will.

Has grief entered your home? Let God be your comfort. His comfort is tailor-made to your pain and your hurt. Let him hold you and bless you. Place your hope in his promise that joy will come in the morning.

Bad Days

"My grace is sufficient for you,
for My strength is made perfect in weakness."
Therefore most gladly I will rather boast in my infirmities,
that the power of Christ may rest upon me.

2 CORINTHIANS 12:9 NKJV

We all have bad days. And some are really bad. We give into selfish desires. We are unloving and impatient. We make terrible decisions and unwise choices. Bad days can make us feel so defeated.

Discouragement is not our friend, is it? Yet, it constantly tries to sneak into our hearts unwelcomed and unbidden. God sees beyond our bad days. Beyond our terrible choices and ugly moments. He sees directly into our hearts, and calls us worthy, despite the mess. He knows us and he loves us.

Are you holding on to bad days? Cast away those days;
name them insignificant and take hold of the grace God gives you.

A Reflection

The only letter of recommendation we need is you yourselves.
Your lives are a letter written in our hearts;
everyone can read it and recognize our good work among you.
2 CORINTHIANS 3:2 NLT

A good measure of how we are living as followers of Christ is to look at the way our children—our greatest assignments—are behaving out in the world. This is not set in stone, and there are special cases where the most loving and competent parents are dealt a season (or more) with a challenging child. But if the parents of our children's friends routinely tell us we must be doing something right, then we must be.

Christ's light can shine in and out of us, and our children reflect that light wherever they go. Well done, moms!

What do other adults think of your children? Spend some time with God in prayer and record what he reveals to you about the reflection you are casting through your children. Where are you shining? Where can you grow?

Simple Treasures

Give thanks for everything to God the Father
in the name of our Lord Jesus Christ.
EPHESIANS 5:20 NLT

The tasks of mothers in and of themselves can be terribly dull. Not everyone can find huge excitement in reading the same story over and over again. We can only take so much mac-and-cheese and finger painting especially when both end up on the floor and we find noodles stuck to our socks while scrubbing red paint out of the carpet.

Motherhood is a gift. It's not to be taken for granted and it certainly should never lose its luster. It's often in the simple moments that we find the most beauty: braiding our daughter's hair when she's just finished her bath, giggling over freshly baked cookies, making tents out of blankets. These are the moments we find our treasures in. Let's be careful not to call them mundane.

Do you feel stuck in the everyday tasks of motherhood?
Look around you and enjoy the simple treasures. God delights in watching you, and he loves when you take delight in watching your children.

At the End of the Tunnel

You are my hiding place;
you protect me from trouble.
You surround me with songs of victory.
PSALM 32:7 NLT

It is such a gift to be able to look back on life and know that it was all part of a plan. No matter the circumstance, it turned out for the best. We can see God's hand in the ups and downs, in the confusion and hurt, in the joy and the pain. While we were in it, it might have seemed unmanageable. It may have been so trying that we couldn't see how we would ever come out on the other end intact. But we did. He brought us there. Learning from that experience is valuable.

We are bound to have more of those moments that seem unconquerable. In those times, we can picture Jesus walking toward us, arms outstretched, pulling us into his embrace. Most often, in those difficult moments, all we want is his comfort, reminding us that it is going to be okay.

What has Jesus brought you through that you can clearly see now? Maybe you are experiencing one of those moments right now. Take heart. God promises to be there in the midst of the chaos. He will bring you through to the other side stronger than you were before.

Needing a Shepherd

"I am the good shepherd;
I know my sheep and my sheep know me…
and I lay down my life for the sheep."
JOHN 10:14-15 NIV

There is a reason Jesus calls us sheep and himself a shepherd. Jesus' original audience was familiar with shepherding. They knew that sheep are some of the least intelligent animals out there. They are weak, prone to wander, and helpless in times of danger. Every sheep needs a shepherd to lead, correct, protect, and provide for them. Jesus wasn't being condescending when he called us sheep; he was letting us know that he wants to take care of us.

Any mother that's honest with herself is keenly aware of her own weaknesses. She doesn't have all the answers. A mother is considered vulnerable because in times of danger, by instinct, she won't protect herself; she will take care of her children. Because of this, she needs a protector. She also needs someone stronger than she is to lean on when she doesn't have all the answers.

Are you keenly aware of your weaknesses?
Jesus wants to be your shepherd.
You do not have to do everything on your own.

The Greatest Commandment

"Listen, O Israel! The LORD is our God, the LORD alone. And you must love the LORD your God with all your heart, all your soul, and all your strength. And you must commit yourselves wholeheartedly to these commands that I am giving you today. Repeat them again and again to your children. Talk about them when you are at home and when you are on the road, when you are going to bed and when you are getting up."

DEUTERONOMY 6:4-7 NLT

In your home, you probably have a long list of rules. There are rules about respect, safety, and morality. What if there was one rule—just one—that made all the others easier to follow?

In Deuteronomy, before Moses gets into the particulars of a very long, specific list of rules from God, he sums it up neatly and simply with this idea: God is God, and he wants us to love him with all that we are. We need to pass this thought along to our children.

What would your life look like if every decision you made started with the question, "Will this show my love for God?" How would it affect your parenting if you taught your children to make their choices this same way?

Careful Attention

*I have no greater joy than to hear that my children
are walking in the truth.*

3 JOHN 1:4 NIV

When we plant a garden in the spring, we don't leave it to flourish by itself. Rather, we water it religiously. We get down on our knees and weed it; our hands dirty and raw. We work the garden with great detail and attention. Every day we tend to the potential garden faithfully; waiting for it to grow. Before long, our tireless efforts are rewarded with sweet fruit.

If we left a garden unattended, it would grow wild. Eventually it would be choked out by weeds. It would wither away and die without the right nutrients. Our lack of devotion can kill the most promising of seeds. God has entrusted us with precious little souls. We are accountable for them. We should be careful to feed them the Word of God, nurture them with love and grace, and protect them from the harsh elements of this world. We need to be attentive to our children's spiritual needs so the world cannot choke them with lies.

How attentive are you to your children's spiritual needs?
Ask the Lord how to nurture your children in every stage of their lives.
You can help them grow strong by giving them what they need:
wisdom from God's Word.

Fragile Yet Successful

*We now have this light shining in our hearts,
but we ourselves are like fragile clay jars containing this great treasure.
This makes it clear that our great power is from God, not from ourselves.*
2 CORINTHIANS 4:7 NLT

If things are working, especially if you find yourself shaking your head and wondering how they are working, you are right where God wants you to be. How did you pull off that school project your child forgot to mention until bedtime the night before it was due? How did the checkbook numbers suddenly fall into place, when only yesterday you had no idea how you'd pay the bills this month?

If we want to be certain God is at work in us, we should consider the rather astonishing fact that we are still standing, still thriving, still rising to another day's challenges when we know without a doubt we can't be doing it all on our own.

Do you occasionally (or even often) find yourself successful despite your own blunders and shortcomings? Praise God for using you, a fragile, possibly cracked pot, to do his great work.

Defined by the Past

He has delivered us from the domain of darkness and transferred us to the kingdom of his beloved Son, in whom we have redemption, the forgiveness of sins.

COLOSSIANS 1:13-14 ESV

Our pasts do not define us. Who we were and what we did before we were saved is irrelevant. Our past does not describe our character or value. In Christ we are a new creation. God is a God who redeems. He takes what is broken, messy, and unclean and makes it new.

We were once sinners, but we have been bought and redeemed by the precious blood of Christ.

Are you enslaved to your past? Let it go. Accept the new life God has given you. Refuse to be weighed down by old choices and patterns. Don't be enslaved to what was. Let your new life in Christ free you.

Change of Season

"Be strong and courageous, and act; do not fear nor be dismayed, for the LORD God, my God, is with you. He will not fail you nor forsake you until all the work for the service of the house of the LORD is finished."
1 CHRONICLES 28:20 NASB

You will, undoubtedly, have various seasons in your life: seasons of longing and contentment, seasons of discouragement and joy, seasons of more and less. Being a grown-up means stretching into new ways of living, and this usually doesn't happen until the season hits.

Seasons can be challenging. They require bravery, obedience, dedication, and sometimes total upheaval of everything comfortable in our lives. If we feel that impending corner of a season change in our hearts, it usually means God is preparing us for something different—a *change*. In those seasons of life, the one who won't change, won't back down, and won't leave us stranded is our heavenly Father.

Do you see an impending season change approaching?
How does it make you feel? Be brave! God will not move you into something without giving you the grace you need to make it through.

Drawn In

Lord, I love the house where you live,
the place where your glory dwells.
PSALM 26:8 NIV

Can you sense God's presence in your home? Does his glory dwell among perfectly dusted and arranged shelves, or among undone dishes and piles of laundry? You don't need stacks of Christian books or Bible verses stenciled on your walls; you don't even need clean walls (or floors, or countertops) to invite God into your home and to feel his loving presence all around you.

God is love. No matter what our homes look like; if they're full of love, he'll be drawn there. And so will others.

Do you want to have "the house"?
The one all your kids' friends come to?
Ask God to fill it with love and watch them come.

Hope in Desperation

We have this hope as an anchor for the soul,
firm and secure.
HEBREWS 6:19 NIV

When was the last time you were desperate for a miracle? Where the circumstances were so dire and all of the facts pointed to disaster? Where your heart cried out for God to come and save you?

In moments of desperation, we have two choices. We can crumble and lose sight of all hope, which, in itself, is a devastating choice. Or, we can choose faith. It doesn't matter how desperate our situation is, we can still choose to believe that God has our best interests at heart. Because he does.

Do you understand that walking by faith is a choice? It's not always the easiest choice though. It may mean leaving your comfort zone, but it always gives God the opportunity to strengthen you. No matter what you come up against, it is hope that feeds your faith.

Selflessness

Each of you should use whatever gift you have received to serve others,
as faithful stewards of God's grace in its various forms.
1 PETER 4:10 NIV

When we choose to live for other people, our lives immediately take
on greater value. We are no longer living for our own benefit but for
the benefit of many. It can be more rewarding to serve others without
concern for what we might receive in return, than to live only looking out
for ourselves. That is not the way we were created. We were created to
love selflessly. Selfless love is shown through directing our time, money,
and effort toward others.

No amount of personal wealth or gain can amount to the reward we
get when we serve others, putting them before ourselves. And what a
valuable lesson we are teaching our children. When we serve without
grumbling or complaining, we are teaching them selflessness. In today's
society, that is a rare skill.

What tangible things can you do to teach your kids selfless love?
Remember that often your children are watching you for an example on
how to live. You can teach without saying a word.

Steadfast Love

The LORD is good;
his steadfast love endures forever,
and his faithfulness to all generations.
PSALM 100:4–5 NRSV

As mothers, the expectation is that we will be full of endless, warm-fuzzy love for our children. However, children have the ability to push us in ways we have never been pushed. They expose things in our hearts that we didn't know were there like control, bitterness, impatience, and anger. *Ungodly things.*

In the moments we stand face-to-face with our weakness and sin, one of the best things we can do is fall on the feet of Jesus. We confess our failures and receive his mercy and forgiveness. Then, we can enjoy his love. His love is altogether different than ours. It is steadfast. It never ceases. It never changes. It never comes to an end. When tested, it doesn't fail.

Does your love feel fickle at times? Don't feel guilty that you aren't like Jesus. Let his love fill your heart. As you receive more of his steadfast love, you will be able to give more to your children and those around you.

Beneficial Correction

*To learn, you must love discipline;
it is stupid to hate correction.*
PROVERBS 12:1 NLT

Just for fun, try this one out on your kids the next time they complain about a deserved consequence. First of all, they'll have to get past the fact the Bible is basically calling them "the s-word," which you have probably banned. But after that, the door will be open to a great conversation.

Have them imagine living with a dog that had never been taught not to chew shoes or to go outside to do its business. You can't grow without failing, and you can't change without correction. It can be hard to convince a child you are disciplining them because you love them. At the time all they know is that something they want, whether an action figure, cell phone, or car keys, has been taken away, and they are not happy.

How do you show your children love when you discipline them?
How does God show you love when he is correcting a fault in you?

Letting Go

Let each generation tell its children of your mighty acts;
let them proclaim your power.
PSALM 145:4 NLT

As Christian parents, we know and believe that even though our children are ours to hold, nurture, and love, they really are the Lord's. There is comfort in knowing that they belong to the one who will go to the ends of the earth to protect and keep them from harm. Even still, letting them grow and letting them go is a very difficult part of parenthood.

Raising children in a self-centered culture is challenging. Letting them out of our protective reach to go into that culture is insanely difficult. But, eventually, it must be done. We can only trust that we have given them tools to be prepared. The best tools are Jesus Christ and his Word. With God, our children have the ability to overcome any temptation that the world hands them.

Do you find it difficult to release your children into the world?
How does knowing that God has already overcome every kind of evil
make releasing your grasp a little easier? When you send your children to
school, to be with their friends, or to pursue their dreams, it's really the
Lord you entrust them to.

Weight of Actions

Humble yourselves before the LORD,
and he will lift you up.
JAMES 4:10 NIV

Have you ever heard the saying, "Do what I say and not what I do?" It is an expression created by parents who knew their children were watching their every move. Nothing gets past our children. They are always paying attention. Our words carry very little weight compared to our actions. Children look to us to see if we are honest, patient, unselfish, and loving. They learn by example. What a heavy responsibility especially when we are bound to make mistakes.

When our words don't match up with how we live, our children are sure to hold us accountable. When they do, rather than giving them the I-am-the-parent-and-you-are-the-kid speech, we should be honest with our shortcomings and admit fault when needed.

Do you find it difficult to humble yourself in front of your children? Because they are watching when you ask for forgiveness, you can confidently live by the words you teach. When you fail, admit it, apologize, and move on.

Influence to Advocate

"Every plant not planted by my heavenly Father will be uprooted, so ignore them. They are blind guides leading the blind, and if one blind person guides another, they will both fall into a ditch."
MATTHEW 15:13-14 NLT

From the day we are cognizant, we begin taking on influences. As parents, we have the huge responsibility of being the primary influence in our children's lives until they make their first friend, step into daycare, or even observe others from inside the shopping cart. And then our responsibility shifts; we take on the role of advocate, getting to know as much as we can about the adults and children our young ones interact with especially those they admire.

Setting our children up for success by giving them as many godly influences as we can is one of the best ways we can love them. Letting them be led by people whose values are not in line with our own is a recipe for disaster, especially as they get older.

What steps have you taken to monitor the influences in your children's lives? Ask God to lead them toward people who love him, and to grant them discernment to avoid those who would lead them down the wrong path.

Joy-filled Journey

*Consider it pure joy, my brothers and sisters, whenever you face trials of
many kinds, because you know that the testing of your faith produces
perseverance. Let perseverance finish its work so that you may be mature
and complete, not lacking anything.*

JAMES 1:2-4 NIV

There is joy in the journey: in the mundane details, in the difficult times,
in the confusing moments, and in the tears. There is so much joy to be
found in the quiet and in the noise.

Pity parties and comparisons create a direct path for the enemy to steal
our joy. But there is hope in Jesus and the gift of little joy-filled moments.
They come in varying forms: little hands and feet, sunshine rays pouring
in the windows, a nice person at the check-out counter, a turn-the-radio-
as-high-as-it-can-go kind of song, a dance party in the living room, the
taste of a delicious meal after a long day, or a movie with the family.
Whatever the moment, there is joy if we look for it.

There's a journey of joy in waking up every day knowing it's another day
to breathe in the cool autumn air, sit outside watching your kids play, or
head to dinner with a girlfriend. Can you find joy in the moment?

October

Surely your goodness and unfailing love
will pursue me all the days of my life,
and I will live in the house of the Lord forever.

Psalm 23:6 nlt

Worthy of Love

"Are not five sparrows sold for two pennies?
Yet not one of them is forgotten by God.
Indeed, the very hairs of your head are all numbered.
Don't be afraid; you are worth more than many sparrows."
LUKE 12:6-7 NIV

You probably didn't change the world today. You probably didn't climb a mountain, make a ground-breaking film, raise a million dollars for cancer research, or author a software application that will make millions of lives easier. Maybe you didn't even make dinner. Or the bed.

So, was your day worthless? Not to anyone you interacted with in love! No matter how small the gesture or how short the conversation. You are important! You are valuable, you are loved, and you are irreplaceable. Believe it.

Are there days you find it hard to believe God could love you fiercely, deeply, and desperately—the way you love your own children? Why do you think that is the case? Ask him to help you believe, and to help you let down your defenses and feel his immense love.

Get Rich Quick

"Do not store up for yourselves treasures on earth, where moth and rust destroy, and where thieves break in and steal. But store up for yourselves treasures in heaven, where neither moth nor rust destroys, and where thieves do not break in or steal; for where your treasure is, there your heart will be also."

MATTHEW 6:19-21 NASB

Advertisements for losing twenty pounds in ten days, getting rich in thirty days, or changing your financial future in three easy steps are all over the place. Marketing companies dangle the schemes and we buy them because they appeal to our desire for a quick-and-easy fix.

Knowing and loving God is not a magic pill that takes away all of our problems. God is not a get-rich-quick scam we buy into. But we will become rich in other ways. Knowing him will fill us with joy and hope. He will give us faith to walk through the darkest of struggles and a heart that is compassionate and loving. He will teach us how to give and serve.

God's definition of wealth differs greatly from the world's. Do you feel wealthy as a child of God? Spiritual wealth is of much greater importance than physical wealth. Store up those treasures that can't be taken away like the joy, peace, and love found in Christ.

Ugly Moments

"The LORD, the LORD,
a God merciful and gracious, slow to anger,
and abounding in steadfast love and faithfulness."
EXODUS 34:6 NRSV

Those who are closest to us get to see us at our ugliest moments. Unfortunately, children are often the recipients of our anger. This is not something to berate ourselves for. It is something to bring to the light of his presence. When our anger is brought to the light, our healing will more quickly appear.

It's important to remember that God is also a parent. As a parent, we know that he is slow to anger and rich in love. When we hear that, we aren't to hate ourselves for our anger. We are to fall down in humility. He will show us his forgiveness and his richness of love.

Have you ever been surprised by your own anger? Don't let this Scripture make you feel worse. It should give you the grace you need to be more gracious to your children. Once you taste again how good God is to you, it will be easier to show your children the same kind of goodness and love.

Significance

You formed my inward parts;
you knitted me together in my mother's womb.
I praise you, for I am fearfully and wonderfully made.
Wonderful are your works; my soul knows it very well.

PSALM 139:13-14 ESV

You are significant. You are significant if you are single or married. You are significant if you have a high-paying job or are unemployed. You are significant if you stay home with your kids or go to work. You are significant if you are an orphan or if you come from a big family. You are significant if you are an extrovert, introvert, or somewhere in between. You are significant because God knit you together in your mother's womb. You are fearfully and wonderfully made.

We are all significant and we matter to God. We can't let anyone tell us differently. God's Word for our lives is the truth that should be impressed on our hearts so it can never leave us.

Do you feel significant? Believe the truth of what God says:
he set you apart and you are wonderfully made!

Loved in Failure

Above all, love each other deeply,
because love covers over a multitude of sins.
1 PETER 4:8 NIV

Peter's first letter is all about how to live as a follower of Christ. Resist temptation in places that are filled with it. Do good and expect to suffer for it. Love your enemy but don't expect any love in return. Sounds fun, doesn't it? Mostly, it sounds impossible. Consider your life as a mother: never give in to cupcakes, clean and organize your child's room, and be yelled at for moving their favorite shirt.

The occasional failure is inevitable, so what do we do? We open our hearts even more to Christ, and we love. We love as much and as well as we possibly can. We love the driver who cuts us off in traffic. We love the angry teenager that used to be our precious, happy child. Peter assures us if we get that one right, the rest of it won't matter so much.

How often do you tell your children you love them? What things, big or small, do you do each day to remind them how much they are loved? Ask the Father to imbed that love deep into their hearts.

Legacy of Life

"You shall love the LORD your God with all your heart and with all your soul and with all your might. These words, which I am commanding you today, shall be on your heart."

DEUTERONOMY 6:5-6 NASB

We are the authors of our own legacy. Each day we are given the opportunity to create our own stories: stories that will be retold in great detail to future generations. A million moments and choices have the ability to impact so many lives. We make choices that create history and determine the future.

Is God woven throughout our stories? We should be diligent in the choices that we make, choosing kindness, love, and patience. Let's make these things our legacy. Let them be what people will remember us by.

What story are you writing today? Let it be a story of love, forgiveness, and redemption. Let it be one that tells the good news of a life in Jesus Christ.

Limited Influence

It is the Lord your God you must follow, and him you must revere.
Keep his commands and obey him; serve him and hold fast to him.
DEUTERONOMY 13:4 NIV

For the first few years of parenthood, we have a tremendous amount of influence over our children. Basically, if we say it's cool, it's cool. If we say something is undesirable, they have no interest. But then it happens. "My friend said everyone watches that show." Or, "I'm the only person in my class that wasn't allowed to go." Following the crowd and fitting in is suddenly a lot more important than following Mom's advice.

As mothers, we're not entirely immune to this, either. We want our children to fit in, to have friends, to be popular. Sometimes, we may even find ourselves getting drawn into the mommy-vortex of competition and gossip; big girls like to fit in too. It can be quite tempting to go along with the majority. Is it really such a big deal if we bend a rule here and there?

Are there situations in your own life or in the lives of your children where you find yourself compromising your beliefs and values? Ask God to show you anything you might be overlooking, and for the strength to hold fast to him even at the expense of your popularity.

A Light Burden

"My burden is light."
MATTHEW 11:30 NIV

Are you burdened with commitments, responsibilities, and worries? What does God have on your plate that you are facing? Jesus said his burden is light. What a precious gift he gives us in that statement! When considering our burdens, a good litmus test we can ask ourselves is, "Do the burdens that are before me feel light or heavy?"

We will have burdens and responsibilities in life. We cannot escape that. But sometimes we are burdened with things Jesus never intended for us to carry. How can we know which ones are from him? We ask, "Is this burden heavy or light?" We know clearly from Scripture that Jesus' burdens are the light ones. If he has placed it on us, we won't be consumed with its weight.

How does your burden feel today? If you realize it is heavy, cast it on Jesus. Let him take care of it. He never intended for you to carry it on your own.

The Black Hole

The humble will see their God at work and be glad.
Let all who seek God's help be encouraged.
PSALM 69:32 NLT

Discouragement is one of the ugliest, most impactful feelings the enemy tries to devour us with. Once we feel discouraged, there can be a snowball effect. Discouragement piles on until we are sucked into a vicious, black hole of lies. The lies tell us this life is all we live for; lies say we aren't enough and never will be; lies make us believe that we'll never get out of the corner we feel backed into.

Listing logical, spiritual truths can quiet our minds. When we start reciting truth, the lies will soon be silenced. If we humble ourselves before the Lord, we are honest about our limitations and we invite him in to take over.

What are some of the ways the enemy tries to flood your mind with discouragement? Grab a pen, a journal, and your Bible, and sit in the presence of the Lord. Start writing out what you know to be true about who God created you to be and the roles he's given you in this world.

A Lying Tongue

*There are six things the LORD hates—no, seven things he detests:
haughty eyes, a lying tongue, hands that kill the innocent,
a heart that plots evil, feet that race to do wrong,
a false witness who pours out lies,
a person who sows discord in a family.*
PROVERBS 6:16-19 NLT

God hates lies. In Proverbs 6, it's ranked right up there with killing, and plotting evil or running toward trouble. In other words, it's a really big deal. No matter how sweet, well-behaved, and eager to please they are, one day your child will lie to you.

The so-called *white lies* of childhood can seem innocent and even humorous (like insisting they didn't eat the cookie through a face covered in chocolate and crumbs), but biblical wisdom suggests we'd do best to hide our amusement and teach them from the beginning how important it is to tell the truth.

How is lying handled in your home? How truthful are you, really? Ask God to show you areas in your heart you might be blind to, and for the wisdom and patience to teach your children the importance of honesty.

The Perceptive Friend

Encourage one another and build one another up,
just as you are doing.
1 THESSALONIANS 5:11 ESV

Do you see that mom at the gym? The one that seemingly has it all together? You should know something; she doesn't. How do you know? Because none of us do. We all carry around our personal struggles and burdens. The friend that learns how to become an expert at recognizing the needs around her is a treasure.

So many of us have learned how to hide pain and grief, but God never intended us to mother alone. He doesn't care for flighty surface friendships. Deep, life-giving, intimate friendships are part of his design. Just as he created us to need him, he also created us to need each other. He created us to serve and support each other in our worst times and in our best.

There are so many ways you can love and serve your fellow moms. Do you know someone in your life that could use an extra dose of love and encouragement today? Put a plan into action and love her. Be the friend that gently unearths her pain and turns it into joy.

Acting in the Spirit

Walk by the Spirit, and you will not gratify the desires of the flesh.
For the flesh desires what is contrary to the Spirit,
and the Spirit what is contrary to the flesh.
They are in conflict with each other,
so that you are not to do whatever you want.
GALATIANS 5:16-17 NIV

It is impossible to maintain a healthy balance in a life of distractions, commitment overload, and false expectations. Inevitably, we fall apart. When we do, as moms, it is usually in the comfort of our own homes with the people we are most accustomed to—our family. We would never dream of falling apart in the outside world.

Falling apart most often looks like losing it: yelling, sighing, throwing things. Whatever your *falling apart* resembles, it isn't biblical. The harm we can do to those around us when we lose it can be great. We hinder their understanding of grace and God's goodness. He asks us to act in the Spirit, not in the flesh.

Are you in the habit of losing it in the comfort of your own home?
Rely on God's Spirit to help you maintain control.
He will give you the strength you need. You just have to ask.

Clear Commands

"This command I am giving you today is not too difficult for you, and it is not beyond your reach. It is not kept in heaven, so distant that you must ask, 'Who will go up to heaven and bring it down so we can hear it and obey?' It is not kept beyond the sea, so far away that you must ask, 'Who will cross the sea to bring it to us so we can hear it and obey?' No, the message is very close at hand; it is on your lips and in your heart so that you can obey it."

DEUTERONOMY 30:11-14 NLT

If there's something you want your child to understand, you explain it clearly and thoroughly, making sure there is no room for confusion. "I'll meet you right here, in this exact spot, right after school," or, "Use this measuring cup when you feed the dog."

God is no different. He loves his children and he wants us to succeed, especially when it comes to pleasing him. His Word tells us over and over what he most desires of us, clearly, repeatedly. "If you want to please me, love me."

Do your children know how to please you?
Ask God to help you communicate your expectations lovingly and clearly.
Do you find yourself wondering how to please God?
Turn to his Word.

Overwhelming Advice

Do not let wisdom and understanding out of your sight,
preserve sound judgment and discretion;
they will be life for you.
PROVERBS 3:21–22 NIV

There are so many voices giving counsel to mothers. Just walk through your local bookstore: the parenting section is huge. Parenting magazines are in every doctor's office, and experts line up on many TV shows. It seems there are scores of people eager to give us wisdom on how to raise our children. What's worse is that many of them say conflicting things. It can be overwhelming.

It is of utmost importance that we exercise discernment in choosing what advice we take but also what advice we listen to. Our number one question in evaluating the advice should be, "Is this Godly wisdom? Is it consistent with the teaching of Scripture?" God promises to give us wisdom if we ask. We should ask him before we ask others and wait for his direction.

Are you overwhelmed with advice? Take a deep breath.
God has called you and anointed you specifically to parent your child.
Read his Word and compare the advice you've been given with that.
If it doesn't match up, forget it.

Choosing Battles

*"Suppose a king is about to go to war against another king.
Won't he first sit down and consider whether he is able with ten thousand
men to oppose the one coming against him with twenty thousand?
If he is not able, he will send a delegation while the other is still a long
way off and will ask for terms of peace."*
LUKE 14:31-32 NIV

Conflict affects relationships. In the parent-child dynamic, most discord is ultimately resolved, and often connections become stronger. However, as our children get older our battles must be chosen more carefully.

Yes, we are the parents and yes, they must respect us, but we also must consider the overall situation. How important is our position? Is their safety or reputation at stake? If so, we stand our ground. If not, we take pause and consider the cost: if we lose, what do we lose? If we win, at what price? Is being right worth severing a thread in our connection? Sometimes, peace or even compromise may be the wiser route.

How carefully do you choose your battles, both in parenting and in the
rest of your life? What are your kids learning about conflict from you?
Pray God will help you be a mother who takes Jesus' advice,
and teaches her children to do the same.

Worth in Busyness

"Many women have done excellently,
but you surpass them all."
Charm is deceitful, and beauty is vain,
but a woman who fears the LORD is to be praised.
Give her of the fruit of her hands,
and let her works praise her in the gates.
PROVERBS 31:29-31 ESV

Being busy is highly valued in our culture. The longer your to-do list and the more filled your appointment book, the more valuable you are. Not busy? Then you must not be important. This is the message we receive.

That message could not be more deceiving. Being busy is not an indication of worth, nor is it a measure of success. In fact, every second of the day can be scheduled with work, activities, and meetings, and we can still be ineffective in every area of our lives.

Where does your worth come from? In God's eyes, your worth is not measured by how much you do. You are special and important simply because you are a child of God. So, if you find yourself over-committing your calendar or saying yes to requests to confirm your value, stop.

Consistent Living

They delight in the law of the LORD,
meditating on it day and night.
PSALM 1:2 NLT

At first glance, this can seem like an impossible standard. Who gathers all their delight from following the rules, or has time to do nothing but meditate on the law of the Lord? But what if that's not what the Psalmist meant?

Do we act one way around our children, another with our friends, another with our Bible study members, and still another around our families? Perhaps the *blessed* the psalmist refers to are those who are consistent: the same Christ-loving, God-fearing version of themselves both day and night regardless of whose company they are in.

Do you feel like a tree planted by streams of water, or are you a little parched? Ask God to help you be the same person day and night, and to let your children see the fruit of a life lived this way.

Humble Attire

*Those who accept correction gain understanding.
Respect for the LORD will teach you wisdom.
If you want to be honored, you must be humble.*
PROVERBS 15:32–33 NCV

Sunday mornings can be totally crazy: showering, finding your best clothes, eating a hurried breakfast, getting everyone in the car on time, all for the love of Sunday church. You get in the car kind of sweaty from the last five minutes of hurried activity, half your kids are crying because you tried too hard to make their hair look nice, and the other half can't understand why everyone had to wear coordinating colors anyway.

Pride. We are all susceptible to it. Maybe we want to walk down the aisle of church looking as if we have everything together. We have to be careful, sisters. Pride and perfectionism go hand-in-hand. Pride can be demotivating for living in simplicity, and perfection is unattainable, making our quest feel meaningless. Instead, we should clothe ourselves in humility.

Do you struggle with perfectionism or prideful behavior? God doesn't expect you or your children to look or to be perfect. He wants you to come to him as you are—the real you. Maybe it's time to let everyone dress themselves and do their own hair this Sunday.

Abiding

"Abide in me as I abide in you.
Just as the branch cannot bear fruit by itself
unless it abides in the vine,
neither can you unless you abide in me."
JOHN 15:4 NRSV

There are many things God doesn't ask of us as mothers. He doesn't ask us to be perfect. It's impossible anyway. He doesn't ask us to be sinless. This is impossible as well. He simply asks us to abide in him in the presence of our children. As we abide in him, many things will rub off on our children.

Abiding in him means not leaving the faith. It means modeling steadfastness for our children when circumstances are shaking. It means repenting to him when we sin. We give our children a gift when we model how to be restored to the Father after we sin. It shows them how to respond when they sin.

Many things will change in the course of your children's lives while they are living in your home. When you continue to walk in God's love and forgiveness, it will make a deep impression on their minds, hearts, and spirits as they grow in him.

Reward of Trust

"My God sent his angel to shut the lions' mouths so that they would not hurt me, for I have been found innocent in his sight. And I have not wronged you, Your Majesty." The king was overjoyed and ordered that Daniel be lifted from the den. Not a scratch was found on him, for he had trusted in his God.

DANIEL 6:22-23 NLT

Once we're past the innocence of childhood, trust is hard to give. We know we're supposed to trust God, and maybe we do, intellectually. But day to day, it can be a real challenge. How early in life did you learn that the world is not entirely safe? The world cannot be trusted, but God can. Some days, believing this can be a pretty tall order.

Few have had their trust in God put to the test quite as dramatically as Daniel, who was forced to spend the night alone with a hungry lion. Logic, reason, and probability all leaned toward an obvious outcome, and it wasn't a good one for Daniel. But Daniel was safe because he trusted in his God. God desires your trust, and he rewards it: sometimes with deliverance, sometimes with peace. It will be okay. You, your children, this problem, this life. It will all be okay.

What is the hardest part of your life to trust God with? Try turning it over to him and claim your reward.

Household of Faith

"If you refuse to serve the LORD,
then choose today whom you will serve.
But as for me and my family,
we will serve the LORD."
JOSHUA 24:15 NLT

These days most homes center around work, school, and extra-curricular activities. The joke that most moms live in their minivans is not far from the truth. Meals are eaten from here to there as we rush from one activity to the next. Little time is given to relationship–building or conversation.

We can easily lose ourselves in day-to-day tasks, so it is important to consider what rules our lives and make adjustments when needed. Having a joy-filled, God-centered life takes effort and planning. There are so many things we can do: family game nights, special meals together, community projects, walks in the park, spring cleaning, and garage sales, to name a few!

What rules your days? Is God at the center of your family?
If not, find ways you can make him a priority in your house.
Don't let activities rule your life.

Teaching Forgiveness

If we confess our sins to him,
he is faithful and just to forgive us our sins
and to cleanse us from all wickedness.

1 JOHN 1:9 NLT

One of the most important things we can teach our children is forgiveness. Whether they need to ask for our forgiveness, or ask it of a sibling, friend, or stranger, it is a biblical virtue that God asks us to practice and teach. Undoubtedly, there have been moments where we have overreacted, or raised our voices a little too loudly, or not shown our children compassion in a moment of weakness; these are opportune times to teach forgiveness.

Asking our children to forgive us isn't easy because it means we have to admit that we were wrong and put ourselves in a position of humility. When we sin, we repent to God and ask for his forgiveness; then we should go straight to our children and ask for theirs. The admittance of error and request for forgiveness will teach them more than all our failures and mistakes.

Do you need to repent of something? Get down on your knees before God and before your children. Look them in the eye and tell them you were wrong. Ask them to forgive you. Teach them what repentance looks like.

On the Surface

"You clean the outside of the cup and dish, but inside they are full of greed and self-indulgence. You are like whitewashed tombs, which look beautiful on the outside but on the inside are full of the bones of the dead and everything unclean."

MATTHEW 23:25, 27 NIV

Is your child's room a mess? If it's pretty clean, check the closet and under the bed. Chances are you'll find a pile or two. Or worse. It takes a great deal of patience and perseverance to teach a child to really deal with their messes instead of merely moving them out of sight.

How about us? This can be literal, in the form of a messy closet or junk room, or it can be more figurative. Do we present a together, happy, organized face to the world while our hearts overflow with clutter, pressure, and disarray?

Spend some time with God today letting him clean the inside of your cup. Bare your biggest messes before him and let him wash you.

Strength in Weakness

He was crucified because of weakness,
yet He lives because of the power of God.
For we also are weak in Him,
yet we will live with Him because of the
power of God directed toward you.
2 Corinthians 13:4 nasb

Becoming a mother highlights our profound weaknesses. We can be ashamed of our weaknesses because they show we aren't perfect, or they reveal that we can't do it all. We get irritated when our children don't obey immediately, respond in anger when they talk back, are easily annoyed when they demand our attention, or become impatient when they are trying to learn something new, and the list goes on.

Our weaknesses aren't there to make us feel bad; they are there so we can enjoy our Savior's strength. Weaknesses force us to run to the cross for mercy. They are a gift of humility that aid us in boasting only in Christ.

When you are conscious of your weakness, you know how strong God is. He isn't asking you to be strong like he is; he simply wants you to be his child.

Truly Listening

*"To those who listen to my teaching, more understanding will be given.
But for those who are not listening, even what little understanding they
have will be taken away from them."*

MARK 4:25 NLT

There's usually a space on a child's report card for "Pays attention in class." We are pleased with positive remarks, glad to know we have a child who listens to those trying to teach them. If we find we have a poor listener, we grow concerned. How, after all, are they going to learn if they don't listen?

Indeed, we would do well to ask this same question of ourselves. Are we hearing God's words without listening? Do we skim over our "daily verse" only to forget it within moments and miss what God might have been trying to teach us that day?

Reflect upon recent struggles or recurring themes in your life.
Is God trying to teach you something right now? Spend several minutes listening for God's voice and write down anything he brings to mind.

Unchanging

*Jesus Christ is the same
yesterday and today and forever.*
HEBREWS 13:8 NIV

Find comfort and rest in knowing that though we live in a world that is in a constant state of change, God remains the same. Babies grow and teenagers go off to college. God remains the same. Jobs change and friends go off in different directions. God remains the same. Health falters and loved ones pass away. God remains the same.

Even though change is not always easy to embrace, you can learn to accept it because God always remains the same. He is constant and steady. He is your rock when everything around you is altered. He remains faithful and his love for you is never ending.

Do you fear change?

Consider the Lilies

"Observe how the lilies of the field grow; they do not toil nor do they spin, yet I say to you that not even Solomon in all his glory clothed himself like one of these. But if God so clothes the grass of the field, which is alive today and tomorrow is thrown into the furnace, will He not much more clothe you?"

MATTHEW 6:28-30 NASB

God gives us plenty of promises in Scripture. He wants us to search them out. He wants us to store them in our minds. When his promises are etched in our memories, they will begin to seep into our hearts.

God explains why we don't need to worry. The reason he addresses this in the first place is because he knows we have a propensity to do just that. But he makes it clear that as his children, worry and anxiety are never necessary. He calls us to consider lilies. Lilies do nothing. If simple flowers are provided for by God, how much more will he provide for his children?

Worried one, how can you stop and consider the lilies today? There is a better way. Hear God's call beckoning you to walk away from anxiety into his provision. Why not rest in that promise instead of worrying?

Heart Posture

"I will teach you to respect me completely, and I will put a new way of thinking inside you. I will take out the stubborn hearts of stone from your bodies, and I will give you obedient hearts of flesh."
EZEKIEL 36:26 NCV

Heart posture. It's a phrase heard among believer friends. *What was the posture of your heart in that moment?* Heart posture takes maturity to understand. For many of us, the act of doing something is usually enough: putting your hands in the air when a convicting song is sung at church, asking for forgiveness because you overreacted, or volunteering at a local charity. But if we were to ask God to show us our hearts in those moments, what would we see?

Would our hearts show we were truly praising Jesus for his ultimate sacrifice? That we were actually remorseful when we asked for forgiveness? That we were serving because we want to love others as ourselves? Our heart posture is what matters in serving God. It shows the true nature of our response.

Meditate on your heart posture as situations arise today. Can you honestly evaluate your motivation in those moments? Be encouraged that God gives you his Spirit to help you keep your motivations pure.

Unique Attributes

If the whole body were an eye, where would the sense of hearing be?
If the whole body were an ear, where would the sense of smell be?
But in fact God has placed the parts in the body, every one of them, just as
he wanted them to be. If they were all one part, where would the body be?
1 CORINTHIANS 12:17-19 NIV

"I wish I were great at lacrosse."

"Why is my hair thin and mousy? I want her hair."

Though your children may be perfect to you just as they are, they may wish they'd been given different gifts, attributes, or circumstances.

In a family with one great athlete, one brilliant mind, or one mane of glorious hair, jealousy and a lack of contentment can easily arise. Helping children see and appreciate their own uniqueness and embrace their own place in the big picture is challenging but worthwhile.

Think about aspects of yourself that you are less than content with. Ask God to show you why he chose to give you those attributes and begin to embrace them. Share your honest feelings with your children; let them see your human side.

The Rules

"God says, 'Honor your father and mother,' and, 'Anyone who speaks disrespectfully of father or mother must be put to death.' But you say it is all right for people to say to their parents, 'Sorry, I can't help you. For I have vowed to give to God what I would have given to you.' In this way, you say they don't need to honor their parents. And so you cancel the word of God for the sake of your own tradition."

MATTHEW 15:4-6 NLT

If your children are old enough to speak, they have probably challenged your rules. Occasionally, their challenges may point out a weakness or contradiction in your policies. This happened to the Pharisees quite often when Jesus was around.

In Matthew 15, Jesus is confronted by some Pharisees who are offended that his disciples don't perform a ceremonial hand washing before eating, thereby breaking a rule. Jesus turns their complaint around on them and points out that in order to follow some of the invented rules of the Pharisees, people must actually break God's commandments. In an effort to maintain order, they'd lost sight of their true priorities.

How often do you butt heads with your children over the rules? Pray and ask God to show you if you have a Pharisaical approach to obedience, or if you are basing your rules on God's law.

Sibling Rivalry

Hatred stirs up conflict,
but love covers over all wrongs.
PROVERBS 10:12 NIV

If you grew up with siblings, you know that siblings have a mutual understanding: fight hard and forgive fiercely. Be honest to a fault, but make sure everyone is okay in the end. Above all else, love. We love each other despite our differences and appreciate how God created us. We embrace the similarities that make us siblings, yet we're sure to point out the nuances that make us unique.

Siblings are a beautiful thing. Big brothers adore and protect, older sisters guide and care, younger brothers are playful and fun, baby sisters are adventurous and sweet. God has a plan for every family, and siblings are a precious gift.

What was your family like growing up? Is the family you have now what you envisioned, or did God have different plans for your life? God has designed your family to fit perfectly together in its own unique puzzle. Embrace what you have been blessed with today.

November

My God shall supply all your need
according to His riches in glory by Christ Jesus.

PHILIPPIANS 4:19 NKJV

Comfort that Remains

God is our refuge and strength,
an ever-present help in trouble.
Therefore we will not fear, though the earth give way
and the mountains fall into the heart of the sea,
though its waters roar and foam
and the mountains quake with their surging.
PSALM 46:1-3 NIV

A warm place by a cozy fire. A cup of coffee with a close friend. A piece of chocolate cake after a long day. All of these things bring comfort, but they can only temporarily pacify an aching heart. And oh, how our hearts can ache. So often we try to fix what is bothering us with comforts of the world. What mom hasn't gone on a shopping spree when feeling stressed? Or indulged in a venti salted caramel mocha to get through the day? Sometimes our search for comfort leads us into scary addictions in an effort to mask and relieve pain.

How wonderful that God is our constant and steady comforter! He is our shelter, our blanket of security, and a hiding place from a scary world. He promises that he will not leave us.

Who do you turn to for comfort? You can cling to the promises in Psalm 46 when you feel sad. All of the world's comforts will fade away. When they do, you can rest assured, knowing God remains.

Band-aids

Children are God's love-gift;
they are heaven's generous reward.
PSALM 127:3 TPT

The price of disposable band-aids varies slightly from company to company. A standard band-aid—one void of any superhero or princess—currently costs about ten cents. However, if we want a kid-oriented band-aid, the price increases considerably. Those range in price from twenty-three cents all the way up to a dollar each. For a disposable piece of plastic that might last half a day (if you're lucky), it seems like a hefty price to pay. Or does it?

When children ask for a band-aid, most of the time that isn't really what they are asking for. If we can listen beyond the tears, the whine, and the urgency, what we will hear is a much deeper question: "Will you stop your day to listen to me, to love me?" Giving our children a band-aid, no matter the cost, shows them that we care. It validates their concern.

Sometimes the little things mean more than the big in the life of a child. Is it worth "wasting" ten cents on a wound that you know isn't bleeding to demonstrate you care? It's not a large investment, but it is guaranteed to pay off in the long run.

Desired Plans

*"Seek first the kingdom of God and His righteousness,
and all these things shall be added to you.
Therefore do not worry about tomorrow,
for tomorrow will worry about its own things."*

MATTHEW 6:33–34 NKJV

The desires of our heart can constantly be at odds with the desires God has for us. When they align, it is a beautiful, peaceful realization. But when they are different, it can create confusion, mistrust, and frustration, often because we lack discernment.

So we pray. We pray that God gives us peace. We pray that his will be done no matter what that means for us. In strict obedience to God, we choose not to be anxious. He promises to guard our hearts. If we start to feel frustrated or anxious again, we pray. So much of life is out of our control, so why do we bother agonizing? We should just pray.

What desires do you have that God hasn't yet shown you?
Can you truly release them to his care, trusting him with your life plan?

Burdened Mother

Without faith it is impossible to please him,
for whoever would draw near to God must believe that he exists
and that he rewards those who seek him.

HEBREWS 11:6 ESV

It is normal for mothers to carry the burden of intercession for their children. They see things that others don't, and they often have longings for their children that the Lord has placed in their hearts.

Ultimately, it's God's work. They are *his* children. We have an invitation to agree with his desires and partner with him in the work that he is doing in our children. That partnering might look different through different stages of life. He might call us to fast regularly for their healing, pray with other mothers, or keep a journal of his promises over our children. Either way, we need to know that it is God's job to care for our children, and ours to have faith as we seek him.

Are you desperate to see a breakthrough in your child? Casting the burden on the Lord is not giving up. It is an act of faith that proclaims, "This child is in the Lord's hands." And faith always pleases God.

Infertility

"I will bless her and will surely give you a son by her.
I will bless her so that she will be the mother of nations;
kings of peoples will come from her."
GENESIS 17:16 NIV

"Now Sarah, Abraham's wife, bore him no children" (Genesis 16:1). It's a simple statement about a very big issue. It fails to communicate the devastating situation Sarah faced. She was unable to fulfill the one duty that gave her worth in her community. It's not unlike how many women feel today in the often hopeless struggle of infertility.

Those who have experienced the pain of infertility need to be assured that God has not left. He has not checked out. He is faithful and loving. He promised Abraham and Sarah a baby boy, and at ninety years old, Sarah bore Isaac. God does not make this same promise to everyone, but through Sarah we learn that God truly is the giver of life, and he can perform miracles! If we allow God's truth to penetrate our hearts, we can also let that truth settle our emotions.

Have you or someone close to you experienced the difficult journey of infertility? Do not mistake God's silence for his absence. His timing is perfect and his plan is good. Remember this in the moments you feel unsure.

Exercising Self-Control

Like a city whose walls are broken through
is a person who lacks self-control.
PROVERBS 25:28 NIV

"Control yourself!" It's an admonishment we hand out freely to our children, but oh, how often we ourselves struggle with self-control. Whether it's refraining from comfort-eating, getting to the gym, or holding a sharp tongue, everyone battles for control in some aspect of their lives. Over and over, the Bible encourages us to exercise self-control. But why? Would it really be so bad if you polished off that bag of sour cream and onion chips? Well, maybe. Kind of. Yes.

A huge part of our job as moms is to teach our kids how to make good decisions: the kind that keep them safe, healthy, and whole. No one needs to control themselves around a bowl of fresh spinach. Self-control helps us say no to things that can harm us. Let this verse shine a little perspective today:

A city without walls is a city vulnerable to attack. Are there areas of your life you are leaving open to ruin? Where do your children need your help in this regard? Ask God to bless you with power over your own struggles and the wisdom to guide your children toward choices that will leave them fortified and strong.

In the Word

Let the word of Christ dwell in you richly in all wisdom,
teaching and admonishing one another in psalms and hymns
and spiritual songs, singing with grace in your hearts to the Lord.
COLOSSIANS 3:16 NKJV

With everything else we have to do during the day, spending time in the Word is usually the last thing we make time for. There is so much that fills our minds that at the end of the day all we want to do is relax. Sometimes reading the Bible seems like work: a discipline to practice or a task to check off our ever-growing list. We often feel guilty that our Bibles lay untouched on the side of the bed, yet we have managed to keep up with the latest season of a trendy TV show.

God's Word is a gift to weary moms. He doesn't want our devotional time to be a burden. His Word is filled with encouraging promises, direction, and comfort. Our minds have great capacity to be filled with the Word of God. We can hide scripture in our hearts so that it will always be there. How wonderful that God created us with an ability to memorize and know his living Word.

Does reading your Bible feel more like a chore than a blessing? All it takes is a few minutes a day to read his Word. Write Scripture notes all over your home: above your kitchen sink, above the stove, on the mirror, and in your car! Receive the gift God has given you in his Word.

Words of Grace

Let your conversation be always full of grace,
seasoned with salt, so that you may know how to answer everyone.
COLOSSIANS 4:6 NIV

How do babies learn to talk? We know this one; it's by listening. And they are listening all the time. Right around the age of two, your child either said or will say something so precocious (and possibly inappropriate), it could only have come from listening to—and imitating—you. It happens to all of us. Our face reddens, and we go about the difficult job of explaining why they shouldn't say something Mama said.

No matter how old or young our children, it's vital we choose our words carefully. A daughter who hears her mother gossiping will likely become a gossip. A son who hears his mother nagging and criticizing often becomes critical himself. Children who continually hear their mother's loving, life-giving conversations will grow up spreading love and life with their own words.

How does it make you feel when your children sound exactly like you?
Are your conversations well-seasoned, inspiring your kids to speak
graciously? Ask God to show you any areas you need to work on,
and thank him for his grace.

Faithful Direction

I will instruct you and teach you in the way you should go;
I will counsel you with my loving eye on you.
PSALM 32:8 NIV

There is no *right* way to arrange a household. Some homes might have a stay-at-home-parent, others have two working parents, and still others have single parents leading the charge. Whatever the situation, passion must be involved for work, for children, or for the home. If that passion has yet to reveal itself, pray.

In order to hear what calling God has placed on our lives, we have to listen. And it can take a while. Fully understanding what God wants us to do with our lives can take years, and certain pieces of our calling might only surface for a season. When our hearts are radically changed, and we become passionate about a possibility, then we might have found a clue to our calling.

What do you think God has set you apart for?
What are you most passionate about?
Be patient. It takes time, prayer, and diligence to discern his voice. Rest assured, Daughter, he has given you passion and he will direct your steps.

Great Faith

Jesus responded, "It isn't right to take food from the children and throw it to the dogs."
She replied, "That's true, Lord, but even dogs are allowed to eat the scraps that fall beneath their masters' table."
"Dear woman," Jesus said to her, "your faith is great. Your request is granted." And her daughter was instantly healed.
MATTHEW 15:26-28 NLT

There's a story in Matthew 15 about a woman with a gravely ill daughter. As a Canaanite, she was not technically part of Jesus' ministry. She calls out to him, begging for help, but he ignores her. She keeps trying.

"I'm not here for you," he tells her. But she keeps trying.

Would you give up easily when fighting for your child's life, or would you persist as the Canaanite woman did? How about for yourself? Can you think of a time you might have given up too soon? When God at first says no, keep trying. He may be testing your faith.

Race of Perseverance

Let us run with perseverance the race marked out for us, fixing our eyes on Jesus, the pioneer and perfecter of faith. For the joy set before him he endured the cross, scorning its shame, and sat down at the right hand of the throne of God. Consider him who endured such opposition from sinners, so that you will not grow weary and lose heart.

HEBREWS 12:1-3 NIV

There are days where life feels like a race. There are a million things to do: relationships to put energy into, groceries to buy, and clothes to fold. There are deadlines, appointments, and expectations. When life feels like a race, sometimes we just want to stop running.

God tells us that there is one thing that matters; he wants us to run the race marked out for us. He wants us to never give up. We persevere, run to win, and fix our eyes on Jesus the whole way through. He is the only one that matters in our race, and he promises if we fix our eyes on him, we will not grow weary.

Are you tired of running the race?
Focus your gaze on Jesus and gain strength.
He is cheering you on, encouraging you to continue and finish well.

Strength Supply

Blessed are those whose strength is in you.
PSALM 84:5 ESV

God wants us to enjoy being his children. When he calls us children, he isn't devaluing us as grown women. He is saying that even though we grow older, we always get to be his children. It's a statement that invites us to enjoy the benefits of being called into his family.

Children are weaker than their parents. This is evident in wrestling matches between parents and their young children. It's almost comical that the children actually think they might win. We all know that the parents are stronger. God wants us to know that he never asked us to be strong. Our *strength* can never come close to his.

Where do you find your strength? God will supply you with the strength you need. Remember that he is the source of it and enjoy the benefit of leaning on someone stronger than you.

Being an Encouragement

May our Lord Jesus Christ himself and God our Father...
encourage your hearts and strengthen you in every good deed and word.
2 THESSALONIANS 2:16–17 NIV

We all need encouragement. Sometimes it comes from unlikely sources like complete strangers, and sometimes it comes from those we love. Either way, encouragement has an incredible impact on our lives. Receiving encouragement is great, but *being* an encourager is scriptural. We know how wonderful it is when, out of the blue, one of our children says, "You're the best mom, ever!" We beam from ear-to-ear and feel like shouting from the rooftops.

Imagine when we whisper praise to God. Imagine how he feels when we shout our thanksgiving to him. God serves us in outstanding ways and he deserves our daily praise, love, and attention. He is the one who deserves our *everything*.

Have you been encouraged by anyone lately? How can you encourage those around you? Remember who deserves the most praise today. Tell God how much you love him.

Child of God

*"Your Father knows exactly what you need
even before you ask him!"*

MATTHEW 6:8 NLT

There are so many benefits to being a child of God. Even in that phrase, *child of God*, our identity and calling are laid out. We are called to be his children. We get to remain in a parent-child relationship with God. That means we receive the blessing of being cared for *all the days of our lives*.

God wants to do his job. It is not an annoyance to him. We were very much in his plan from before the beginning of time. He awaited our arrival with great expectation and never grows weary of loving and providing for us. Our job, as laid out in Scripture, is simply to seek him.

How do you feel about letting God take care of you?
He is the most stable provider you will ever know.
Let him worry about taking care of you. He enjoys it.

Rusty

Blessed be the God and Father of our LORD Jesus Christ!
By his great mercy he has given us a new birth into a living hope
through the resurrection of Jesus Christ from the dead.

1 PETER 1:3 NRSV

When you bring your car into a repair shop for an oil change and come out two weeks later with $2000 in charges and brand-new parts under your hood, you realize you may have been neglecting a few things. Your car hasn't run this well since you first bought it. All it took was some care, time, and new parts.

We all need newness at times. Newness brings rejuvenation and renewal of our hearts and minds. There is so much hope that comes from a God who promises us new life and refreshment when we seek his face first. It doesn't matter how long we've been getting rusty, or how old or broken our parts, he welcomes us with open arms and a promise of unconditional love.

Do you feel a little rusty?
Ask Jesus to make you feel alive again.
He knows exactly what to do to make you feel new.

Completely Content

*"Seek the Kingdom of God above all else, and live righteously,
and he will give you everything you need."*
MATTHEW 6:33 NLT

Picture a sleeping baby: belly full, diaper dry, pajamas snug. That happily snoozing bundle of love is the very picture of contentment. For now. Until the diaper fills or the belly empties, all is right with the world because all the baby's needs are met. It's so simple when we're small, when our children are small.

The more we grow, the more we want. We want things so badly that we think we need them. And it's not just things we crave, is it? We long for time to read, for kids that don't fight, for our favorite jeans to fit. These longings can steal our joy, and God doesn't want that for us. He desires true contentment for each of us. In fact, he longs to give it to us. All we have to do is look for him and desire him. He promises to take care of everything else.

When is the last time you felt completely satisfied with your life? How long did that feeling last? Try writing out your blessings or keeping a daily gratitude journal. Ask God to fill you with a spirit of contentment that only he can give.

Insecurities

Whom have I in heaven but you?
And there is nothing on earth that I desire other than you.
My flesh and my heart may fail,
but God is the strength of my heart and my portion forever.
PSALM 73:25-26 NRSV

Insecurities have a way of rising up, breaking the surface of our weary souls. They are known to whisper lies in the dead of night: we aren't worthy, we are disappointments and failures, we don't amount to anything. These insecurities leave us broken and empty. We are taught that brokenness equates to unworthiness; weakness is ugly and should be hidden. We are led to believe that a perfect life is a holy life.

But if we paused long enough to let God's words seep into our hearts, we would come to know that it is in our weakness that he is strong. In our brokenness, we are beautiful. In our imperfections, we come to know his grace. His truth has the power to break down every insecurity that we have.

Are you letting insecurities get you down? With Christ, you can rise up against the lies and be confident that you are loved and worthy. Let his truth wash over you today.

Hustle and Bustle

*May the Lord of peace himself give you peace
at all times and in every way.*
2 Thessalonians 3:16 niv

Hustle and bustle. It can easily relate to the life of a mom. There are always things to do, and as our kids grow that list doesn't get shorter. We hustle when they are little because we are chasing them around. We hustle when they get older because they are involved in school, sports, and social activities. But it doesn't have to be that way. It really isn't about what's on the list; it's about what's in our hearts.

If we can't spend time playing with our kids, or we're signing them up for activities to keep up with those around us, it is time to examine our hearts. There are choices we can make that create less hustle and bustle for the people that matter most to us. It might mean saying no to activities and yes to quieter evenings at home. It feels good to say yes to the things that really matter in life.

Are you in a perpetual state of hustle and bustle? Start to find joy in the quiet things again. It will revitalize you and lift up your spirit when you're on the ground tickling your kids or curled up with popcorn and a movie.

Prayer Life

"Where two or three gather in my name,
there am I with them."
MATTHEW 18:20 NIV

The prayer life of Jesus is inspiring. Like so many things, he lays out a model worth following. First, he prayed privately (see Luke 9:18). As busy moms, it isn't always easy to find the time, but we must realize that God is always available. He hears our every thought, so time is not an excusable factor. Prayer should be a top priority not a last resort.

Second, the ninth chapter of Luke goes on to mention Jesus praying in a group setting (see Luke 9:28). Our relationship with God is personal, and Jesus encourages us to get alone to pray, but he also wants us to pray with others. We could find prayer groups, get some friends together, or pray with our kids. We should pray with other believers even when it isn't comfortable. Prayer is an important part of worship.

How is prayer an active part of your day?
Do you need to take more time to pray alone or with other believers?
Make conversation with Jesus a regular occurrence in your life.

A Thankful Life

Give thanks to the LORD of lords,
For His lovingkindness is everlasting.
To Him who alone does great wonders.
PSALM 136:3-4 NASB

When life is difficult, it is hard to see beyond our present situation. We become clouded with the trials we face, making the things we have to be thankful for dim. If we take off the glasses of despair and set our hearts on searching for God's fulfilled promises, we will find them.

In every trial there is something to be thankful for: a child's laugh, a cozy house, a beautiful day, a warm embrace, a comforting friend. Focusing on the good in our lives brings light and joy into even the direst of circumstances. Cultivating a heart and attitude of thankfulness brings us strength to press on despite the obstacles that surround us.

Are you struggling to see the good in your life? Sometimes you might need the Lord's help to remind you of your blessings. Start out by writing a list of all you have to be thankful for and make it a discipline to count the blessings in your life.

Being Thankful

"A good man brings good things out of the good stored up in his heart,
and an evil man brings evil things out of the evil stored up in his heart.
For the mouth speaks what the heart is full of."

LUKE 6:45 NIV

"I don't make enough money." "My house is too small." "I hate my job."
Sound familiar? We are so accustomed to grumbling, that complaints drip
off our tongues like rain in a thunderstorm. Even when times are good
and blessings surround us, we take on the role of insolent and ungrateful
children. It becomes a habit to disregard all of the blessings God has
given us. We stomp our feet and demand more.

Complaining turns our hearts cold and bitter. Focusing on the negative
only robs us of a joyful and happy life. When we focus on the positive,
our hearts are changed. Our attitudes are contagious. When we choose
contentment for our homes, it will become a place of peace.

Do you have a grumbling spirit?
Pay careful attention to what you say today.
What is your heart saying about its condition?

Thankfulness

Every good gift and every perfect gift is from above,
and comes down from the Father of lights,
with whom there is no variation or shadow of turning.

JAMES 1:17 NKJV

Cultivating a thankful heart is learning to recognize his perfect gifts: his presence, his grace, his mercy, his love, his healing, his salvation. These are just some of his gifts. They can only come from the Father. They are perfectly designed by him for us. We may long for earth-like gifts, but those gifts eventually lose their luster. They are corruptible.

Gifts from God have eternal value. He knows what you really need, and he gives abundantly.

Can you trust God to give you what you need? Do you thank him for all that he has given already? Write down some gifts God has blessed you with recently and determine in your heart to be thankful.

Praising God

I will give thanks to the Lord with my whole heart;
I will recount all of your wonderful deeds.
I will be glad and exult in you;
I will sing praise to your name, O Most High.

PSALM 9:1-2 ESV

Have you ever noticed how taking the time to praise God seems to change everything? We are admonished to praise God in all circumstances. We have an entire book of the Bible filled with poems that were actually songs when they were written. God knows that when we praise, our hearts are filled with encouragement and joy.

We give our children a gift when we sing or play worship songs in the home. As we praise God, we remind ourselves of his attributes. We remember his love, and our hearts are encouraged. Children perceive this. Sometimes they don't have the words for why their hearts are heavy, but a mindful mother can help point them to Jesus simply by singing with, or over, them.

Did you know that sometimes it is a discipline to sing? You won't always feel like it, but as you step out and thank God purely because he is worthy, you will find that your heart will follow your actions.

Joy Stealer

Always be thankful.
Let the message about Christ,
in all its richness,
fill your lives.
COLOSSIANS 3:15 NLT

As moms, comparison can quickly become a joy stealer. *Her kids act so much better than mine. Why are they able to move and we're still stuck in this financial mess? How can she always look so put together and I'm in pajamas every day? I am still driving this old car and she got another new one. No way did she have all those babies; I don't even look that good and I only have one!*

Once we start comparing, it becomes really difficult to stop. When we focus on the negative, that is all we end up seeing and feeling. How sad it makes our Father when we constantly live in a state of thinking we are unworthy! In order to change a heart of comparison, we need to cultivate a heart of gratitude.

Who do you constantly compare your life to? How does it make you feel when you put your life against theirs? Oh daughter, he has much bigger plans for your heart! Start changing your way of thinking and focus on the areas you feel grateful for. He wants you to feel joy in thankfulness.

Gift of Thanksgiving

Give thanks in all circumstances;
for this is the will of God in Christ Jesus for you.
1 THESSALONIANS 5:18 ESV

Are you experiencing some trying circumstances? In some ways, we all are. No one is immune to sorrow and suffering when they are on earth. However, God does not want us to be consumed by our circumstances. He gives us a simple, yet extremely powerful tool that will aid us in walking through our painful circumstances—the act of thanksgiving.

God intends for us to pause and give thanks no matter what our circumstances. Sometimes it's a discipline to find something to be thankful for. We might have to grit our teeth and say *thank you*, but as we do, we notice that our hearts begin to follow. Gratitude drives back the clouds of darkness and despair. It is how persecuted Christians walk in joy when they are in chains. When we start thanking God, we realize that even in suffering, he is there. And if he is there, then we never have to be afraid or alone.

Can you find something to thank Jesus for in the middle of your hardship? Break the habit of complaint that is so common and walk with a heart of thanksgiving.

Counting Blessings

You make known to me the path of life;
you will fill me with joy in your presence,
with eternal pleasures at your right hand.
PSALM 16:11 NIV

Every good thing comes from God. We've heard this, and we know this, but how often do we really ponder it? Take some time and consider every positive aspect of your life. Think of your children, home, extended family, friends, vocation, hobbies, and more. Think of every great decision you ever made, every hunch you followed to success. Every good thing.

Now consider God, your Father; he has given you all of it. That's how much he loves you.

When was the last time you listed out your blessings?
How has the list grown or changed since then?
Count your blessings today and let God fill you with joy and gratitude.

Faithful Attender

O taste and see that the LORD is good;
happy are those who take refuge in him.
PSALM 34:8 NRSV

We serve a glorious God who likes to move us with his Spirit! He awakens our souls and puts a seal of love on our hearts. We might have days where we feel his presence constantly: the feeling of being alive, wanting to love, and knowing we're forgiven and free. If we could, we would grab hold of Jesus, our hands entwined with his, and never let go. Then, the next day comes with its distractions, and everything from the previous day is forgotten.

God is faithful. He remains. He shows up again and again. His presence is a *fact* not a *feeling*. The fullness of his presence comes at us, and our hearts feel alive, our tear-filled eyes spill over in joy, and hope is ours again. What a patient, loving, faithful Father we serve. Only he could keep showing up, awakening our spirits, and igniting a fire of love for him.

Where have you felt the presence of God?
If you search for him, he can be found in everything.

The Money Ladder

Command those who are rich in this present world not to be arrogant nor to put their hope in wealth, which is so uncertain, but to put their hope in God, who richly provides us with everything for our enjoyment. Command them to do good, to be rich in good deeds, and to be generous and willing to share. In this way they will lay up treasure for themselves as a firm foundation for the coming age, so that they may take hold of the life that is truly life.

1 TIMOTHY 6:17-19 NIV

We are abundantly blessed. It isn't always easy to see who is truly *rich* or *poor* because in the western world our viewpoint is skewed. If we own a car and even part of a house, we are some of the richest people in the world.

No matter where we are on the economic ladder, God asks us to do good, be generous, and put our hope in him. He will provide everything for our enjoyment. By holding true to these virtues in our lives, we lay a firm foundation for the coming age.

Do you know you are abundantly cared for? Think through times where God has come through for you financially. This life is temporary. Do good, be generous, and put your hope in God. True living comes later.

Imperfection Exposed

*You were taught, with regard to your former way of life,
to put off your old self, which is being corrupted by its deceitful desires;
to be made new in the attitude of your minds; and to put on the new self,
created to be like God in true righteousness and holiness.*
EPHESIANS 4:22-24 NIV

We all have our weaknesses. Showing our children that we make mistakes and always need a Savior helps them recognize the same is true for them. Living an authentic grace-filled life gives our children freedom to do likewise. We don't want them enslaved to the lie that they have to hide their faults. They need to know they can be authentic and live in the light.

It is inevitable that we will fail our children and disappoint the people around us that we love. We are not perfect. We lose our patience (time and time again), withhold mercy and love, or choose selfishness and pride. But we can learn how to embrace our mistakes and humbly ask for forgiveness, or we can deny our shortcomings and give the false illusion that parents are perfect. Doing so is destructive.

Are you living an authentic life before your children? If not, they will constantly strive for impossible standards and never learn how to rest in the truth that God loves them regardless of their mistakes. Accept his grace for you and give your children freedom to do the same.

It's Not Fair

"Don't I have the right to do what I want with my own money? Or are you envious because I am generous?"

MATTHEW 20:15 NIV

Jesus tells a wonderful story in Matthew 20 about a landowner who goes into town early one morning to find workers for his field. He agrees to pay them a fair daily wage. On four occasions throughout the rest of the day, he goes back and hires more workers. At the end of the day, he lines them up. Those he hired last are paid first and receive the daily wage. Those who had been working all day assumed they would get more, but when their turn came they were given exactly what they were promised. "But that's not fair!" they complain.

"But that's not fair!" If there is more than one person in your house, this accusation will surface. If you have more than one child, it will surface often. As hard as you try, discipline, attention, and even love are difficult to distribute evenly. When in doubt, follow God's example and err on the side of generosity.

How do you feel about fairness?
Share your thoughts with God.

December

Faith is the confidence
that what we hope for will actually happen;
it gives us assurance about things we cannot see.

HEBREWS 11:1 NLT

Giving Is Better

*Whoever oppresses the poor shows contempt for their Maker,
but whoever is kind to the needy honors God.*

PROVERBS 14:31 NIV

Have you ever served with your children at a local charity and watched their faces as they wrestle with the fact that they are giving basic food to a child who gobbles it up like it's a Thanksgiving meal? Or maybe they've helped pack a basic meal into a baggie knowing it is going to kids overseas who will eat the same thing every day without complaining.

If only we adults could still grapple for understanding like our children do! With more and more negativity on the news—murder, theft, abandonment, abuse, starvation—God's desire for us is to have a heart that knows to give is better than to receive. Our lives are richer when we do things for those who have less.

Where can you start serving the poor? If you have an opportunity to share your wealth, give your time, or share your talents, do it. If you have space in your house, fill the empty rooms. If you have extra, give it away. Bring honor to the Lord by giving of yourself.

Lovable

By this we know love,
because He laid down His life for us.
1 JOHN 3:16 NKJV

One of the biggest lies Satan tries to feed us is that we are not loveable. We aren't worth fighting for or saving. We are expendable and easily replaced. He taunts us with the sins we have hidden in our hearts, and we feel ashamed. We become unable to lift our eyes to face our loving Father and accept the grace that he freely offers.

God deems us worth saving. So much so, that he sent his only Son to die for us. In that act, Father, Son, and Spirit forever abolished the lie that we are unlovable.

When was the last time you called yourself unlovable?
Don't reject the priceless gift of the cross. Let yourself see the love that was poured out for you in that moment and for all of eternity.

I Don't Know

*I don't really understand myself,
for I want to do what is right, but I don't do it.
Instead, I do what I hate.*

ROMANS 7:15 NLT

When our children misbehave, we typically have one burning question. *Why?* Sometimes, the answer is immediate and obvious. "I punched her because she made me mad," or "I ate all the cookies because they were really good." Other times, and far more often, we hear, "I don't know." We persist. There has to be a reason. *Why did they do it?* The infuriating "I don't know" comes back again and again. Why? Because it's true.

Do we understand all our own sins? The apostle Paul earnestly addressed this problem in his letter to the Romans. Having a healthy understanding of sin's place in our lives is vital if we are to teach our children to recognize its place in theirs. Not so we can make excuses for ourselves, but so we can realize our utter dependence on Jesus to free us from our sins.

Spend some time reflecting on your most baffling, frustrating, and recurring sins, then take them before God and lay them at the cross. You may have to do this over and over, but that's the beauty of the Gospel. You can. Jesus and his love for you are not going anywhere.

Disappointments

This hope will not lead to disappointment.
For we know how dearly God loves us,
because he has given us the Holy Spirit
to fill our hearts with his love.
ROMANS 5:5 NLT

Most moms have stories of disappointment. Maybe something extravagant was planned and it didn't turn out as hoped: a failed birthday party, an expensive vacation that got rained out, or a promised present that was sold-out at the store. Parental disappointments come in many different forms. Despite the frustration, these can actually become great opportunities for us and our children.

As mothers, we want to protect our children from the pain of disappointment. We are doing them no favors by shielding them from it though. Disappointments are a huge part of life, and we have the opportunity to teach our children how to process them when they come their way.

Can you think of a recent time when your child was disappointed and how that made you feel? Do you know that God can use all disappointment to produce great things in the heart of your child? Mostly, you can expect him to help teach perseverance, character, and hope. And hope is something that will never disappoint.

Beauty Defined

Don't be concerned about the outward beauty of fancy hairstyles, expensive jewelry, or beautiful clothes. You should clothe yourselves instead with the beauty that comes from within, the unfading beauty of a gentle and quiet spirit, which is so precious to God.
1 PETER 3:3-4 NLT

When you look in the mirror what do you see? Often we are better at pointing out our "flaws" than acknowledging the beauty that is there. Motherhood is not always glamorous. We feel worn out and tired. But those tired eyes we critique tell the story of a devoted mother who selflessly gives her life to her children. That servanthood is beauty.

True beauty goes deeper than what we can see in the mirror. We may not feel beautiful according to the world's definition, but to God our beauty is unsurpassable.

When you look in the mirror do you feel beautiful? Can you see how your service to your children is precious to the Lord? When he looks at you, he sees the inner beauty of a mother's heart.

The Grower

Neither the one who plants nor the one who waters is anything,
but only God, who makes things grow.
The one who plants and the one who waters have one purpose,
and they will each be rewarded according to their own labor.

1 CORINTHIANS 3:7-8 NIV

Paul's letters to the churches he founded often read like letters from parents to children who have gone out into the world on their own. As such, we can glean some great parenting advice from him. In his first letter to the Corinthians, Paul addresses some division among the members regarding whether they consider themselves his followers or that of Apollos. Paul quickly sets them straight: they follow God.

Your children aren't really yours. You get to plant and water the seeds, but ultimately it is God who makes them grow, and he determines who they will be.

Spend some time thanking God for the opportunity to nurture one of his precious chosen ones, and ask him to show you where you can grow.

Grace for All

The LORD God is our sun and our shield.
He gives us grace and glory.
The LORD will withhold no good thing
from those who do what is right.
PSALM 84:11 NLT

"I think I'm bad, and I just want to be good, Mama." That will tug at our heartstrings. Those words were the detrimental confirmation we were hoping would never come. We suddenly realize that with every disappointed shake of our heads, every sharply delivered word, every exasperated sigh, our children were feeling smaller and smaller.

There is hope, mothers—hope to turn it all around. We can change the behavior of our children by encouraging them. Instead of overreacting to an accident, we can show them how to clean up the mess they made. We lead by example. Children learn empowerment from doing things on their own without us hovering over them. We can show them the love of God by giving them endless amounts of grace. Most importantly, we can't look back. Let's keep our eyes focused on the prize, move forward, and start over every day.

Can you start to see your children as God sees you? Encourage them, praise them; show them your love in hugs, positive words, and gentle reminders. There is enough grace for everyone.

Never Alone

Be content with what you have, because God has said,
"Never will I leave you; never will I forsake you."
HEBREWS 13:5 NIV

It's amazing how even in a house full of children we mothers can feel a deep sense of loneliness. Among the chaos and noise, we still long for the presence of God. We may not always feel him, but in the midst of everything around us, he is there.

You can attempt to fill the void with so many things. God is the only one that can meet your needs, and he will if you let him. When you feel alone, remember that he promises to never leave you.

Ask God to fill your heart and home with his presence today.
He will not leave you.

Intelligence Match

A person's wisdom yields patience;
it is to one's glory to overlook an offense.
PROVERBS 19:11 NIV

When your two-year old stomps her foot and demands that you are wrong, it might take everything in you not to burst out laughing. When she does the same thing at six, it's a little less cute. At twelve, it's irritating. And at sixteen, it's downright maddening.

When older children challenge our intelligence, why does it cause such a reaction in us? It really has nothing to do with the child and everything to do with our *need* to defend ourselves. It's in these moments that we have to choose not to be offended or react out of our own insecurities. It might be easy to beat our children in an arguing match, but what does that really accomplish? Instead we can teach our children the art of answering offense with gentleness and grace. It's something they will benefit from greatly as they grow older.

Can you remember today that God is your defender?
He is more concerned about the state of your heart
than who wins the argument.

Watched

*"I have the right to do anything," you say—
but not everything is beneficial.
"I have the right to do anything"—
but not everything is constructive.
No one should seek their own good,
but the good of others.*

1 CORINTHIANS 10:23-24 NIV

A mature believer understands that actions do not determine salvation; when we accepted the sacrifice of Jesus Christ on the cross, we were adopted into God's family and assured a place with him in heaven. But in his first letter to the Corinthians, Paul reminds all of us to consider our actions in light of how they may be perceived by others.

As mothers, we understand there are little eyes watching our every move, basing their view of the world, and of Christ, on what they see us do and hear us say.

What are your children learning about the heart of a Christ-follower by watching you? Is there something different you would like them to see?

Jars of Clay

Now, O LORD, you are our Father;
we are the clay, and you are our potter;
we are all the work of your hand.
ISAIAH 64:8 ESV

Depending on the age of our kids, most days as a mom are spent making food, cleaning up that food, washing clothes, putting away clothes, getting kids dressed, picking up toys, and playing referee to the squabbles of siblings. Some days taking a shower seems like the most daunting task, let alone spending time with the Lord.

But oh, the renewal and peace we get when we sit in obedience to our Father, letting him fill our spirit with his love and gentle words. He says we were created as jars of clay, clay that can be molded and reshaped into something beautiful and unknown. If left out, that jar of clay can dry out and crack, thirsting for moisture. God promises us his abundance and peace, quenching our very driest parts.

When do you feel most renewed? Wherever you are right now in your walk, God hears your cries for renewal, your whispers of longing for his peace to fill your soul. Take time today to be refreshed by his Word and sit with him in prayer.

Temporary Suffering

The God of all grace, who called you to his eternal glory in Christ,
after you have suffered a little while, will himself restore you
and make you strong, firm and steadfast.
1 PETER 5:10 NIV

Life is filled with much joy, but sorrow and suffering are woven into each story. We face tragedy and great lost. Sometimes we suffer from physical or emotional pain that threatens to destroy us. Perhaps mental illness has taken a hold and we can't see an escape route.

The afflictions of this world are deep and burdensome. We cry out to God asking why and plead for him to save us. We can take comfort in knowing that when we're in Christ, all suffering is temporary. We may feel crushed, but we are not. God promises to rescue us.

Do you feel God's presence in your suffering? You don't even have to search for God; he is already there walking beside you, and he's ready to carry you when you feel you can't go further. Rely on his steady arms to hold you and bring you through your difficult situations.

Holding His Hand

Children, obey your parents in the LORD, for this is right.
"Honor your father and mother"—
which is the first commandment with a promise—
"so that it may go well with you
and that you may enjoy long life on the earth."
EPHESIANS 6:1-3 NIV

We try to teach our kids to value others above themselves, honor God above all else, and respect themselves enough to stay pure and true to who they are. Unfortunately, today's world doesn't make that very easy. It isn't the world we grew up knowing; it doesn't always offer grace, or second chances, or do-overs.

But Jesus does. He promises a clean slate in repentance to him and it's important to teach our kids that he will never abandon that promise. They are bound to make mistakes, whether big or small, and we want to send them off into the world everyday knowing Jesus is there holding their hands.

Do you have an opportunity to sit down with your children and speak about honor? It's great for you to also communicate that God never leaves us or forsakes them. He doesn't count their sins against them but forgives them. That is a beautiful truth, isn't it?

God Is Watching

The LORD looks down from heaven and sees the whole human race.
From his throne he observes all who live on the earth.
He made their hearts, so he understands everything they do.
PSALM 33:13-15 NLT

Do you remember the first time someone told your childhood-self that God was watching you? Like, all the time? Maybe this thought brought you comfort and maybe, like a naughty child being reminded that Santa was making his gift-giving decisions, you were a little bit intimidated by this news. Mostly, the reaction to the reality of a God who is always watching depends on current behavior and the condition of the heart.

It's not so different for us today, is it? God saw us get up extra early to make breakfast and pack lunch for our children today; check one off in the "nice" column. God saw jealousy darken our heart as we listened to a friend recount her trip to Hawaii. Uh-oh? Mercifully, no. God sees us, but he also knows us. He knows we are not perfect; that's not why he's watching. He's watching us for the same reason we love to watch our children: he loves us!

What does God see when he looks at you?
List out the things he loves about you, his precious daughter.

Creating Margin

*Our people must learn to devote themselves to doing what is good,
in order to provide for urgent needs and not live unproductive lives.*

TITUS 3:14 NIV

Are you in a pattern of always saying yes? Afraid of letting others down?
As mothers, this is an easy trap to fall into. We want to say yes to our
kids when they ask to have a friend over, yes to our family when they're
arranging dinner plans, yes to our friends when they want to hang out,
and yes to that special event or awesome opportunity. Yes feels good,
until it doesn't.

When we long to say no, when we crave a moment of peace after the
kids are in bed and the dishes are put away, that list of yes items can
seem like an unattainable mountain. Constantly saying yes leads to an
exhausted mom and less than our best. Carrying that feeling around is
much worse than choosing to say no. Making time for ourselves and our
family is admirable. Desiring more margin in our lives for simplicity is
okay; that is something to say yes to.

In what areas of your life do you crave more margin?
Pray for the courage to say these words when you need them:
"No thank you, we've got enough on our plate right now."

Desperate for Rest

It is useless for you to work so hard
from early morning until late at night,
anxiously working for food to eat;
for God gives rest to his loved ones.
PSALM 127:2 NLT

More often than not, mothers climb into bed at night bone tired. Being a mom is exhausting. Our eyes close with the hope that tonight we will have a few hours of uninterrupted sleep.

Mothers never get to go off the clock. Not when they are tired. Not when they are sick. Not when the days are long and they are overwhelmed. But God does promise to give us rest.

Do you feel tired? Ask God to provide rest and relief. You can trust in his promise to provide all that you need including supernatural rest. Even when you feel stretched beyond belief, he is there. He will give you the grace and strength you need to make it through the day.

Ride of Trust

Trust in the Lord Yahweh forever and ever!
For Yah, the Lord God, is your Rock of Ages!
ISAIAH 26:4 TPT

You might be a mom who needs to have your days planned months in advance because you like to know what's coming. You knew you would be married at twenty-four, have kids by twenty-six, and be done with your family by the time you're thirty. You imagine your family being raised in a certain house, in a certain city, driving a certain car. You like to dream, to plan, and to know what to expect.

That lifelong plan might come crashing down if God asks us to do something unplanned in unchartered territory. When he steers us in a different direction, it can bring a rollercoaster of emotions. That rollercoaster becomes part of our journey. Hopefully, at the end of it we come out with one emotion stronger than the others—trust. When we trust whole-heartedly in the Father who adores us, we can let go and enjoy the ride…wherever it brings us.

Has the Lord taken you somewhere unexpected?
What experiences have you had that have caused you
to trust in the Father and his plan for your life?
Remember, he loves you unconditionally and he is good.

All Things

We know that in all things God works
for the good of those who love him,
who have been called according to his purpose.
ROMANS 8:28 NIV

This is a truth no mother wants to confront: your child will experience bad things. Heartbreak, failure, loss, and pain are all part of life on earth. We can wish and even pray for this to be false, but to be human is to suffer.

Rather than fear these times and dread their arrival, we can store up the powerful words of Romans 8:28 in our hearts. What an incredible promise! No matter what happens, no matter how bleak or sad the situation, God will bring forth something beautiful from it.

Reflect upon your past pain and look for the good God was able to produce from it. Share your honest feelings with him about your children's future and let his promise give you peace.

Necessity of Food

"I am the living bread that came down from heaven.
Anyone who eats this bread will live forever.
This bread is my flesh, which I will give up
so that the world may have life."
JOHN 6:51 NCV

We would never dare to send our kids to bed or to school without nourishment. They need a well-balanced diet to get through the day. They also need spiritual nourishment. We pray for them and give them opportunities to worship and read God's Word. Our desire for them is to be healthy and strong, so we feed them everything they need in both areas.

But how often do we allow ourselves to go without spiritual food? We too hunger for God's Word to feed us and need his presence to strengthen us. Parenting on empty will eventually lead us to burn out. We must make sure we are being fed.

Are you hungry for God's Word? Take some time to relish in the rich depth of his wisdom and love for you. His food will satisfy you and make you whole. There's no better food than that!

Gift Giving

*Then make me truly happy by agreeing wholeheartedly with each other,
loving one another, and working together with one mind and purpose.
Don't be selfish; don't try to impress others. Be humble, thinking of
others as better than yourselves. Don't look out only for your own
interests, but take an interest in others, too.*

PHILIPPIANS 2:2-4 NLT

Give away your gifts. You probably feel like you do that every day as a mom. While it can be tiring, it is also truth. We might not feel like we are the best moms. We feel like we could do a better job respecting and loving others. We have moments of weakness. But God has given us gifts! He intricately designed us with specific purpose.

God asks us to be selfless. Giving away our gifts and doing everything for others can be exhausting. But God wants us to do it with joy. If we, as moms, daughters, and friends, can find our gifts, embrace them, and use them, we will see God's purpose.

Do you know the gifts the Lord has given you?
Are you using them for his glory?
You will find joy in sharing your gifts with others
when you give them away expecting nothing in return.

Blessed to Give

You yourselves know that these hands of mine have supplied my own needs and the needs of my companions. In everything I did, I showed you that by this kind of hard work we must help the weak, remembering the words the Lord Jesus himself said: "It is more blessed to give than to receive."
ACTS 20:34-35 NIV

There are lessons in the Bible so simple and true we can easily lose sight of their meaning. "It's better to give than receive," we say, without even thinking. To an average two-, nine-, or sixteen-year-old, is this true? Even the most emotionally and spiritually mature teenager may struggle with happily giving all their savings away instead of buying the latest gadget or trendiest new outfit.

We may even struggle with this one ourselves. Sure, it feels great to donate and to volunteer, and we love giving gifts to our children. But aren't there days we'd really just like a new pair of boots, earrings, or maybe even golf clubs? How do we apply Paul's words?

Perhaps the answer lies in the word blessed. Paul never implies Jesus said it was more fun. To be blessed is to be given divine favor or protection. How can you share these thoughts with your children?

Minimal

*Remember that the Lord
will reward each one of us
for the good we do.*
EPHESIANS 6:8 NLT

A more simple life. A life with less clutter. A life with less to-dos. A life where less is more. A life of margin. A life, simply put, less busy. All of these we might desire for our family, and yet, we have a really hard time getting there. As families with young kids, teens, or adult children, there is a laundry list of responsibility not allowing much room for margin.

It is okay to be happy with a calm life. It is okay to *un-busy* your very busy life. It is most definitely okay to start using the word *no* more often. Hopefully on the other end of this very busy life, we will find less stress, less anxiety, and less disappointment.

Do you consider your relationship with Jesus your greatest treasure? He doesn't focus on whether or not you are signing your kids up for the right activities. His desire is your heart. He wants time with you, which means creating a simpler life so you can hear his whisper.

Left with a Gift

"I leave the gift of peace with you—my peace.
Not the kind of fragile peace given by the world,
but my perfect peace.
Don't yield to fear or be troubled in your hearts—
instead, be courageous!"

JOHN 14:27 TPT

Are gifts your love language? Does receiving a gift communicate love to you? The form we like to receive love in is often the same form that we give it. If this is true, then it would seem that one of God's love languages is giving gifts. All throughout Scripture, we read of him giving gifts or rewards to his children. Sometimes the rewards are unmerited and sometimes they are earned, but the concept of gift giving seems to start with God.

What a gift from God! Because he is your maker, only he can know exactly what gift will mean the most to you. He knew that the gift of authentic peace would be not only what you wanted but also what you needed. He doesn't give the same type of gifts you can get from this world. He gives what cannot be destroyed, broken, or misplaced—the gift of his peace.

How can you actively accept God's gift of peace
as you go about your day?

Perfect Present

*"You parents—if your children ask for a loaf of bread,
do you give them a stone instead?
Or if they ask for a fish, do you give them a snake?
Of course not! So if you sinful people
know how to give good gifts to your children,
how much more will your heavenly Father
give good gifts to those who ask him."*

MATTHEW 7:9-11 NLT

Think back to the last time you surprised your child with a gift. Most likely, you went to the store excited to pick out the perfect item. Maybe she mentioned her desire for something specific, but you know your child so well that it is easy to choose something that will please her. You take the gift home and carefully wrap it in secret. You choose the perfect paper all the while anticipating the moment you get to present the gift to her. As she unwraps it, you take joy in her delight; you're happy to share her pleasure. It's wonderful to give.

Now think back to a time in your life when you were blessed: your wedding day, a promotion, the birth of your child, a new house. All of these are wonderful blessings from God. But God is the greatest gift ever. He is present in those moments, relishing in your joy and excitement.

Like every good father, God rejoices with you, celebrating the good things in your life. Invite him in. What gifts did he bless you with this week?

Declaration of Love

"God did not send his Son into the world to condemn the world, but to save the world through him."
JOHN 3:17 NIV

Have you ever considered what happened in heaven on the day earth received the greatest gift in the history of *forever*? When Jesus became a man, he set aside the indescribable power of being fully God and instead embraced humility and weakness.

For a time, the Father lost the immeasurable depth of relationship with his Son and had to watch as Jesus learned obedience through suffering. There is truly no greater sacrifice than what both Father and Son made to declare to us all that we are loved.

Without the work of the Holy Spirit, the incarnation of Jesus would not have been possible. It is the same Spirit at work in you who reveals God's deep love and offers you the opportunity to receive his gift. Can you think on that as you celebrate the season of giving?

God's Plan

*Then he went down to Nazareth with them
and was obedient to them.
But his mother treasured all these things in her heart.*

LUKE 2:51 NIV

We all have hopes and desires for our little ones. We dream from their infancy about who they will become. We send them to the best schools and enroll them in the right extracurricular activities to set them up for the most successful future possible.

What happens when what we have planned for them is not what God has planned? We can let go of our desires because God's plans for our children go far beyond what we could ever imagine for them.

What dreams do you have for your children? Are you okay with letting those dreams go if it means that they will be in the center of God's will? You can rejoice in releasing your children and watching them grow into the people God intended them to be.

His Gifts to You

Let love and faithfulness never leave you;
bind them around your neck,
write them on the tablet of your heart.
PROVERBS 3:3 NIV

Read Proverbs 3:3 quickly and it sounds like another command. Keep loving others; stay faithful. But what if we spend a little more time with it and begin to see that love and faithfulness are his gifts to us, gifts he never wants us to be without.

Bind God's love around our necks; write his faithfulness on the tablet of our hearts. Next, we do the same for our children. No matter where they are, they will never be alone.

Think of three ways God has proved his love and faithfulness to you. Do you carry that proof with you everywhere you go? How can you give your children the assurance that God's faithfulness will never leave them?

Abounding Grace

Let us then approach God's throne of grace with confidence, so that we may receive mercy and find grace to help us in our time of need.
HEBREWS 4:16 NIV

There are moments when we mothers are on our last nerve. We are sick of disciplining, of being backed into a corner, and we just don't know what to do. In those weaker moments when we feel like we could cry, yell, or just give up, we can look at that face staring back at us and think of God's grace. We can remember all the times we've failed, and how it feels when he gives us grace.

Looking into the eyes of the child who has angered us, we silently pray, *Help me in this moment, Father; give me grace.* As we allow him to move through us, we can respond with a hug instead of crying, yelling, or hiding in the bathroom. What a gift it is to have a Father who forgives and forgets, who loves us despite our shortcomings, and whose grace and love for us never runs dry.

Think of how it feels when you get down on your knees in repentance and you are washed clean. Think of the repeated moments of grace he has gifted you with, asking for nothing in return. Can you give your children the gift of grace as well?

Taking Account

*"Where your treasure is,
there your heart will be also."*
Luke 12:34 NIV

A financial advisor would ask you to take account for every last dollar spent over the course of three months. The reason for this exercise is to clearly show our priorities. Where does our money go? Once we know, we can readjust our spending according to our overall financial plan.

The same method could be applied to parenting. Where do we spend our time? If we tracked the time we invested into our relationships with our children, would we come up short? Do we seek God? Do we spend time in the Word? Do we go to church to worship him with others? When we feel like our relationship with God is lacking, it is good to evaluate where we devote the majority of our time and focus.

What things take up your time? Is God a priority in your life? Maybe you need to adjust your priorities or manage your time better so you can invest in your relationship with him. The payoff is well worth it.

God's Love

For God so loved the world that he gave his one and only Son,
that whoever believes in him shall not perish but have eternal life.
JOHN 3:16 NIV

John 3:16 might be the most well-known verse in the Bible. From televised sports to restroom graffiti, it's been engraved in our brains. But have we really wrapped our minds around it? Have we taken into our hearts the incredible depth of his love for us? Every so often, we should read this verse like it's the first time we've ever seen it.

As a mother, it's easy to imagine darting into traffic, leaping into a raging river, or even sprinting into a burning building to save our children. In light of the sacrifice you'd make for your child, consider the sacrifice that was made for you.

How can you make a point to remind your kids of the sacrifice Jesus made for you and for them today? Do they know how much God loves them? Do they know how much you love them? Have you told them lately?

Power of Praise

Jehoshaphat appointed men to sing to the LORD
and to praise him for the splendor of his holiness
as they went out at the head of the army, saying:
"Give thanks to the LORD
for his love endures forever."
2 CHRONICLES 20:21 NIV

In 2 Chronicles 20, King Jehoshaphat faced a huge army of enemies who could have easily destroyed his people. What he did next was quite strange. With a declaration that his eyes were on God, he sent in a choir. In a time of dire crisis, King Jehoshaphat praised God with singing! That army of enemies was out to destroy King Jehoshaphat and his people like the enemy prowls around looking to destroy us.

We need to be aware of the enemy's schemes and evil plans; he is extremely manipulative. We can resist him by praising God for his love and faithfulness. We should praise him for everything under the sun, so when we are faced with an army of enemies, we can boldly walk to the head of the army and declare God's love.

Are you in the habit of praising God even in times of trial? Start small. Begin praising God in your home. Teach your children to praise him for everything they have been given. Thank God for giving you a new year to love and serve the children in your life.